Oct. 25, 1992

For Åke and Helene,

With love and best wishes
and warm Thoughts always,

After Great Pain

A NEW LIFE EMERGES

Diane Cole

SUMMIT BOOKS

NEW YORK · LONDON · TORONTO
SYDNEY · TOKYO · SINGAPORE

SUMMIT BOOKS

SIMON & SCHUSTER BUILDING

ROCKEFELLER CENTER

1230 AVENUE OF THE AMERICAS

NEW YORK, NEW YORK, 10020

COPYRIGHT © 1992 BY DIANE COLE

DESIGNED BY EVE METZ

MANUFACTURED IN THE UNITED STATES OF AMERICA

1   3   5   7   9   10   8   6   4   2

LIBRARY OF CONGRESS CATALOGING IN PUBLICATION DATA

COLE, DIANE.

AFTER GREAT PAIN: A NEW LIFE EMERGES/DIANE COLE.

P.   CM.

1. LOSS (PSYCHOLOGY)   2. ADJUSTMENT (PSYCHOLOGY)   3. GRIEF.

I. TITLE.

BF575.D35C65   1992

155.9'37—DC20   91-25491

CIP

ISBN: 0-671-74944-7

Grateful acknowledgment for permission to quote is made to the following sources:

The poem "After Great Pain" by Emily Dickinson from *The Complete Poems of Emily Dickinson* edited by Thomas H. Johnson. Copyright 1929 by Martha Dickinson Bianche; Copyright © renewed 1957 by Mary L. Hampson. Reprinted by permission of the publishers and the Trustees of Amherst College from *The Poems of Emily Dickinson* edited by Thomas H. Johnson, Cambridge, MA; The Belknap Press of Harvard University Press, Copyright 1951 © 1955, 1979, 1983 by President and Fellows of Harvard College.

Quotes from "The Impact of Parental Death on College-Age Women," by Phyllis R. Silverman, published in the September 1987 issue (Vol. 10, No. 3) of *Psychiatric Clinics of North America*, are used by permission of W. B. Saunders Company.

The quotation from Patricia Conway and Deborah Valentine's article, "Reproductive Losses and Grieving," in Deborah Valentine, ed. *Infertility and Adoption: A Guide for Social Work Practice* (New York: Haworth Press, 1988) is used by permission of The Haworth Press, Inc.

ACKNOWLEDGMENTS

I OWE a special debt of gratitude to all the people who so generously offered to tell me their stories. I also am grateful to the psychologists and counselors I interviewed and especially to Don Scharf, who took many hours from his professional schedule to explain his views on the psychological impact of loss. I also thank Ilene Stargot for being so candid in discussing the "invisible" loss of infertility.

My editor, Ileene Smith, and my agent, Susan Lee Cohen, deserve more than thanks for their unstinting support of and faith in this project. I also would like to thank Laura Wolff, who provided editorial wisdom, encouragement, and friendship throughout; Wray Herbert, who made generous and thoughtful editorial suggestions; and Roberta Israeloff, whose friendship and support were invaluable. Lucille Ettienne and her watchful care of Edward allowed me to complete this book; along with Sharon Headley and Nathaniel Sobel, they provided a special link between playground and word processor.

This book is in many ways a personal tribute to the love and

ACKNOWLEDGMENTS

affection I feel for my mother and father, my brothers and their families, my husband's family, and many friends. It also is an expression of the great joy we have all felt in my son, Edward. Most of all, it is a tribute to my husband, Peter Baida, whose enduring love and strength will always give me reason to care.

For Peter, for Edward,
and for my mother,
Roselda Katz Cole, 1916–1975,
with deepest love and gratitude, always

After great pain, a formal feeling comes—
The Nerves sit ceremonious, like Tombs—
The stiff Heart questions was it He, that bore,
And Yesterday, or Centuries before?

The Feet, mechanical, go round—
Of Ground, or Air, or Ought—
A Wooden way
Regardless grown,
A Quartz contentment, like a stone—

This is the Hour of Lead—
Remembered, if outlived,
As Freezing persons, recollect the Snow—
First—Chill—then Stupor—then the letting go—

—EMILY DICKINSON

CONTENTS

PREFACE

EﾠACH LOSS opens a void within us. It may always remain a part of our inner landscape, but gradually, as the loss recedes, we learn to see it as part of a larger terrain.

For the moment, however, the emptiness stretches ahead, and there seems to be no way to fill it.

I began this book as an autobiographical and reportorial exploration of the psychological impact of loss, but it is my hope that it will serve also as a many-faceted guide to the journey through grief, both for the bereaved and for their friends and families. To some, the book at first may seem a curious hybrid—part memoir, part research and analysis. But there are several reasons why I have chosen to inter- weave my own story with the stories of other people, and to intersperse these in turn with an examination of psychological theory.

Individual memoirs are powerful, but they remain only one person's story. Psychological theory can engage us intellec- tually, but even the most brilliant abstractions sound faint next to the rending immediacy of the mourner's cry. Neither

11

perspective by itself is sufficient; both are needed: the stories to touch and heal us where we hurt; the theory to explain not only why we hurt but how we can begin to heal.

This is a book about grief, but it is also a book about healing. For that reason, I not only recount the actual stories of how people begin to learn to live again; I also place those individual examples in the larger context of how the work of psychological repair takes place. In this way I have tried to show how, in the aftermath of any loss, we begin to reexamine and redefine ourselves, our values, and our possibilities, until a new life emerges.

My own experience of loss and threatened loss lies at the core of this book. First there was the death of my mother, from cancer, when I was twenty-two. Only the year before, while still a college senior, I helped my boyfriend, Peter (now my husband), through his own bout with radical cancer surgery, radiation treatments, and chemotherapy. Coming one on top of the other, these battles—one successful, the other not—left me raw and numb, utterly weary, but perhaps, I hoped, also a little bit wise.

I had mourned the loss of others, but then, one spring morning less than two years after my mother's death, I faced the possibility—what seemed at that moment the probability —of my own bizarre and violent death when an armed band of Hanafi Muslims seized the B'nai B'rith Building in Washington, D.C., where I worked, and held more than one hundred of us hostage there. During those thirty-nine hours of captivity, I grieved for myself and for all I had left undone, but I also came to a new understanding of life's peculiar resilience even amid terror and anguish.

It was thus with even greater joy that, shortly afterward, Peter and I married at last. But even as I began to formulate this book, there came the increasingly apparent reality that, after two wrenching pregnancy losses and a variety of other medical difficulties, I would not be able to bear a child. And although pregnancy loss and infertility are in some ways intangible losses, they nonetheless proved a lengthy ordeal that

12

left me feeling, at my lowest point, less like a woman than like a useless, empty womb.

So many losses clustered so closely together in adolescence and young adulthood may be unusual. "How could you bear to live through so much sadness, much less write about it!" people would ask me.

But each experience of loss also eventually led to a transformation. After great pain came numbness, anger, guilt, and all the other stages of grief, in what seemed an endlessly protracted jumble that defied the stately, ordered march that popular wisdom had led me to expect. And then, finally, each time a new self emerged, one with a different vision of who I am, a different sense of what I could do or even wanted to do, and a different perspective on what my future might hold— as a woman, daughter, wife, lover, and now, finally, an adoptive mother.

After great pain, a new life emerges: That is the theme that weaves itself throughout this book, but it does not belong to my story only. For the journey through loss is one we all have taken or will take. If we're lucky, the story of that journey is a story of renewal. It is a story that reveals how, after great pain, we struggle, cope, and go about the hard business of trying to live again.

/

AN OUT-OF-SYNC LIFE

THE TERRIBLE INITIATION BEGAN during the winter vacation of my senior year of college. I was spending a quiet evening with Peter, my boyfriend for the past four years, when I put my hand to his cheek and felt something hard and round, like a pea. "What is it? What's wrong?" he asked. Silently, I guided his hand to the spot. He sat bolt upright, his dark eyes widening, as he probed. He said nothing. The next week we had an answer to our question, though: It was a tumor, almost certainly malignant. The surgeon recommended extensive surgery, radiation therapy, and chemotherapy, all as soon as possible. Peter was twenty-three years old.

The operation occurred on January 31, 1974. Six months later, even as Peter was slowly making his way to recovery, my mother took to her bed, complaining of fatigue. Emergency surgery revealed that it was something more: cancer of the colon. It had already spread to her lungs and liver. The prognosis was terminal.

Even now, as I remember that time, an abyss opens before me. As I put myself, in memory, once again beside Peter in

15

his hospital bed, then next to my mother as she lay dying, the very ground on which I stand no longer seems secure: Take one step more, and you, too, may fall into the void—a chasm as dark and empty as the world before the world was created.

Grief is indeed a separate world, I discovered then. Knowledge of it will set you apart, at least for a short time, and perhaps forever. Many essayists proudly identify themselves as being part of a generation—"the baby boom generation," "the beat generation," "the post-boomer generation." But after living through Peter's illness and then mourning my mother's death, all before I had turned twenty-three, I never again felt comfortable placing myself as part of any generation at all. As a college senior and then as a graduate student, while my classmates were engaged in the festive excitement and frenzied professional worry of going out into the world, I found myself absorbed with activities of another order: first, in commuting every two weeks from my dormitory room in Cambridge to Peter's home in Baltimore, to cheer him on as he slowly recovered; then, as my mother slowly faded, in traveling from my graduate classes to her side every day, to care for her and to let her know I cared.

That is how my out-of-sync life began.

———

As I go through the letters and journals from the time of Peter's illness, I am struck by the sense of remeeting my younger self, a *Doppelgänger* in time: Here is someone full of hope, energy, and the earnestness of young adulthood—and also the occasional silliness of an almost grown child not entirely ready to say goodbye to adolescence. Here also is someone whose feelings are complicated by the fact that she is quite clearly in love with a young man just two years older than herself who might be dying.

This is what I read and what I remember: On the afternoon of Peter's first visit to the surgeon after the lump was discovered, my mother and I attended a play. We had been going to play and concert matinees together for as long as I could remember, and this was to have been our special winter vacation treat—*The Waltz of the Toreadors*, with Eli Wallach and Anne Jackson. But I don't remember the plot, not a single line of dialogue; I only remember coming home and running to the telephone to call Peter and find out what the doctor had said. The phone rang without an answer.

Nervously, I waited. Driving home from the theater in Baltimore's rush hour, I had almost plowed into the red Buick that edged just in front of us on the expressway's entry ramp. Mom had sucked in her breath and said nothing, acknowledging with clutched hands that her daughter's mind was on other things.

I dialed again, and this time Peter answered. "Hello?" The soft sound of his baritone voice comforted me. If he could speak clearly and without tears, then everything must be all right. "I love you," I said. Like the child I still was, I wanted to babble about the play, about the book I had to read for my final exam next week, about anything but what I had called to ask him: "What did the surgeon say?"

I could hear him trying to decide what to say, what not to say. "I'll be right over," he said.

"It wasn't good, was it?" I said. "It's cancer, isn't it?"

"I'll be right over," he repeated, and added softly, "I love you, Diane."

As I waited for Peter to drive the ten-minute ride from his parents' house to mine, I fought against thinking about the movie *Love Story*. I remembered how, just the year before, I had made fun of the corny story of Ryan O'Neal's unstinting love for the dying Ali MacGraw. How unbelievable the whole thing was, I had announced to my family in my capacity as the budding (and therefore unbearably arrogant) young critic. But the characters in the corny movie had met and fallen in love as undergraduates at Harvard and Radcliffe, just as Peter and I had done. And now I hated the movie even more because their story was starting to turn into our story, and that simply could not be.

When Peter arrived, he told me that the surgeon hoped this

story would turn out better, but in the meantime a difficult road lay ahead. The surgery would be extensive and complex, requiring the removal of a facial nerve and part of his jawbone, as well as various skin grafts from his chest and thighs. When all the cutting was done with, he would have a different face.

"Oh, Peter!" The face that gazed on me with loving sadness was a handsome one, with pale ivory skin, large, questioning brown eyes, and a dark thick brush of a mustache. I touched his cheek again, and he touched mine.

He told me more of the details—the radiation and chemotherapy, the long recovery ahead, and the tentatively hopeful prognosis when all of this was done. There seemed nothing to say beyond that but to cry and to embrace and to declare that we loved each other, that nothing could ever change that, no matter what his face looked like and no matter what the scars. "Are you all right, Diane? I love you, Diane. I'll take care of you, Diane." Peter was the one whose life was in danger, but he was the one who was comforting me.

I know now that every child, however old, needs comforting, but it wasn't until I received a phone call two or three days later that I realized that in the real-life drama in which I now found myself, I could no longer play the child—that in fact I was suddenly not a child at all. "Diane, this is Mrs. Baida," the taut voice of Peter's mother announced. It was a voice that declared immediately who was speaking—an unassuming but intensely caring woman in her mid-forties whose only child was gravely endangered, and consequently so was she. "Peter is on his way over to see you, and I'm calling you now because I wanted to speak to you when I knew you weren't with him."

She paused, then hurried on urgently. "Peter is worried about you, Diane. But Peter needs to worry about himself. I know this is hard for you—it's hard for all of us! But you've got to let him know that you'll be all right, because right now he needs to concentrate on just getting better himself. Diane, you've got to keep his spirits up!"

For the past several days, I had been walking around in a world of heightened unreality; every word, gesture, movement, sound had taken on an exaggerated quality, as if I had walked through an invisible screen and become a player in someone else's life. How odd, I remember thinking, that growing up, I had wanted to write plays, and in high school I had tried out for a part in every drama production. But the intensity in the voice of Peter's mother went beyond any directorial command I had ever heard. I had won the part—won Peter's heart, as he had won mine. Now there was a tragic twist to the plot, and my role (along with everyone else's) had changed radically. Could I adjust? How would I adjust?

A studious sort, I had no preparation, no research to fall back on, no book to consult. Now Peter's mother was telling me: "You've got to keep his spirits up!"

We take our cues, learn to grow up, from many sources. As I go through the letters I wrote to Peter that year—a letter or postcard almost every day—it is clear that I took my task seriously. In letter after letter, I hear the determinedly breezy tone of someone whose optimism cannot be quashed, no matter how grave the news is. Then, more and more, as I grew, there is a deeper resonance of care, concern, and tenderness. "Dearest," I wrote in May from Cambridge, at the end of that winter and spring of surgery and radiation, "From you have I been absent in the spring." The words were Shakespeare's—a far cry from the punning adolescent sensibility with which I had begun our correspondence in January.

By then I had become a different person from the terrified girl who had discovered the lump on Peter's cheek on a winter night that already seemed a lifetime ago. Throughout that worried semester, my final one as an undergraduate, I had found myself taking a far different course of study from my classmates. And at the end of it, I was graduating with a different kind of degree. "I made you grow up," Peter said jokingly one night.

It is only in memory, though, that the many scenes, steps,

and hesitations that made up that transformation blend together, as if that transformation happened all in one terrible jolt. Time had moved quickly and yet unbearably slowly from the moment of discovery to the surgery itself and then through all the stages of Peter's treatment and recovery. Each discrete shock had always come so quickly upon the next, there had never seemed time to act—only to react, to play the particular role called for at the moment, and to do it as well as I could manage and with as much strength, love, and conviction as I could find.

And so, really, each step along the way was a small initiation in itself, none more so than visiting Peter in the hospital intensive care unit—seeing him for the first time after the operation had taken place.

Meanwhile, Peter had of course been undergoing various transformations himself. He would have to learn to live in doubt, he had confided to me—as someone with uncertainty dangling like a sword above his head. The sword read "Cancer," and by extension, it hung over my head, too.

But that particular sword would have remained invisible to others had it not been for the far more visible signs of his ordeal. The operation, we both knew, would leave radical, conspicuous scars: Because of the tumor's location, just below his ear, a facial nerve would have to be cut, and without that nerve, Peter would lose control over the muscles on the right side of his face. That meant that when he smiled, it would be a crooked, left-sided smile only; the other side would remain motionless and seemingly emotionless. Neither would Peter be able to raise his right eyebrow with the questioning, warmly skeptical glance I had come to know so well. Moreover, part of the jawbone itself was to be removed, along with the lower tip of his earlobe. Finally, when all was done, there would be scars on his chest, even on his thighs, as a result of the skin grafts that the surgery required.

This description, in the abstract, sounded ghastly. When Peter emerged from the surgical bandages, what would his "new" face look like? When he gazed into the mirror, what would he see? What sadness or terror would I see when I looked into his eyes? And what would he see reflected in mine?

The date set for the operation was the same day as my final exam in Walter Jackson Bate's famous course "The Age of Johnson." The exam could not be postponed, and so I had traveled back to Cambridge and attempted to immerse myself in the eighteenth-century world of Samuel Johnson, Joshua Reynolds, and Edmund Burke. It would be a losing battle, I was sure, but instead it was a revelation.

Reviewing Johnson's philosophical novel, *Rasselas*, I came across a passage I had forgotten—one that had seemed irrelevant when I first read it in October but that now took on sudden urgency. For this is how the philosopher Imlac comforts the Princess Nekayah after what she believes to be the irrevocable loss of her much-loved companion, Pekuah:

"The state of a mind oppressed with a sudden calamity," said Imlac, "is like that of the fabulous inhabitants of the new created earth, who, when the first night came upon them, supposed that day would never return. When the clouds of sorrow gather over us, we see nothing beyond them, nor can imagine how they will be dispelled: yet a new day succeeded to the night, and sorrow is never long without a dawn of ease. But they who restrain themselves from receiving comfort, do as the savages would have done, had they put out their eyes when it was dark. Our minds, like our bodies, are in continual flux; something is hourly lost, and something acquired. To lose much at once is inconvenient to either, but while the vital powers remain uninjured, nature will find the means of reparation. Distance has the same effect on the mind, as on the eye, and while we glide along the stream of time, whatever we leave behind us is always lessening, and that which we approach increasing in magnitude. Do not suffer life to stagnate; it will grow muddy for want of motion: commit yourself again to the current of the world. . . . "

Johnson, I recalled from my lecture notes, had written this novel in the days just after his mother's death, to help pay for the funeral expenses. Imlac's words were probably designed not only to comfort the Princess but also to bring solace to Johnson himself. Now they consoled me, too—particularly since Johnson allows Pekuah and the Princess to be happily reunited some pages later. For me, too, there would be pain, but it would be followed by reunion and happiness, I thought, and I allowed myself to hope that this story, not *Love Story*, would be mine, after all.

After my exam, I waited restlessly for the phone to ring. Finally, at a little after six o'clock, it did. The operation had taken seven hours, Peter's mother told me in an exhausted voice, but the surgeon was optimistic. Nonetheless, after such extensive surgery, Peter would have to remain in the intensive care unit for the next few days. I told her I would see her —see Peter—as soon as I could get to Baltimore.

Peter's father greeted me at Baltimore's train station the next afternoon with a silently hopeful embrace, then drove us the short distance to Johns Hopkins Hospital. As we passed, first, the red-brick downtown row houses that Baltimore is famous for, then the increasingly shabby, boarded-up buildings of the inner city, Peter's father gave me the latest progress report. Peter was pretty doped up on painkillers, but (or maybe because of it) his spirits seemed remarkably good. He was sleeping a lot, which was also good.

"Good, good." I nodded.

Then he paused and said, carefully, "Are you nervous?" Peter was wrapped up like a swami, his father told me, with his head and the whole right side of his face covered with bandages. There were also a number of tubes and other surgical coverings on his chest and thighs. Then Mr. Baida said, "The way to have courage is to say to yourself, 'I have courage.'" After a minute, he added, "Another thing that helps is to have one or two things ready to say when you go in. That way, you'll be prepared, no matter what you see or feel."

His words, spoken quietly, always carried force, and never more so than now. In the years since, I have often remembered those words as some of the most practical and touching advice I ever received. Perhaps like Samuel Johnson, in speaking to me Peter's father was also counseling himself.

And so, as we walked through the high-ceilinged hospital lobby, past the enormous statue of Jesus Christ designed to give comfort to all who enter there, then through the dreary corridors, smelling of sour antiseptic, I went about writing my script. Peter, I knew, had always found far more solace in a gallows humor that acknowledged the uncertainties of life than in the falsely cheerful pronouncements that "everything will be all right." He was also so avid a Muhammad Ali fan that I had recently taken to calling Peter "Champ," as I watched him channel more and more of his anxiety over his operation into worrying about Ali's upcoming rematch with Joe Frazier.

"Here we are," Peter's father said at last, and pointed to the gray-white door that read "Intensive Care Unit." Sucking in my breath, prepared for everything and for nothing, I walked through the swinging door, entering still another world. I let out the words before the nightmare vision had fully registered: "Hey, Champ, you really got beat up this time!"

It was impossible to look without blinking. Here was the man I loved transformed into someone I did not quite know—his arms shackled to tubes, his head and face covered by bandages, his chest and thighs swabbed with a yellow sponge covering that, in my first shock, I mistook for the insides of his body. "Oh, my love!" I cried inwardly, beating back tears. The side of his face that was not bandaged—that was still Peter—smiled faintly, and the eye that was open fluttered wearily. Quietly, I took his hand; his grasp was weak, but his touch remained warm. "The doctors say you'll be ready to go back into the ring before long, Champ," I said, stroking the back of his hand—almost the only part of his body unencumbered by coverings and thus the only part I could touch. Then,

still more quietly, I said, "I love you, Peter. I'm here." And
again: "I'm here."

———

Every season, whether of joy, worry, sadness, or happy expectation, has a way of taking on its own special tone, as
identifiable in memory as a familiar song. You may not remember every verse or even the exact words to the refrain,
but the meaning and, more than that, the mood are unforget-
table. Not long after Peter's operation, this season, too,
began to develop its own poignant timbre—a soft, somber,
wounded cry that would gradually fade and, I prayed, turn
into something else.

Meanwhile, another rhythm marked the days and weeks of
my semester. Every two weeks, I would take the all-night
train from Boston to Baltimore for a three- or four-day weekend visit with Peter. My train was called "The Night Owl,"
and on those nine-hour journeys I myself came to feel like
some surreal creature, out of sync with a world used to traveling in daylight, out of touch with the various college cares I
was leaving behind—farther and farther behind, as the endless jostling of the train seemed to dramatize just how far
apart my two worlds were.

Armed with countless back issues of newspapers and magazines—*The New Yorker*, *Ms.*, *The New York Times*—along
with various books whose words I would read and reread
without taking in a single thought, I would curl into a fitful,
dreamless sleep, punctuated by the conductor's throaty cries:
"Providence!" "New Haven!" "New York, New York! There
will be a fifteen-minute stopover in New York!" "Trenton!"
"Thirtieth Street, Philadelphia, the only stop in Philadelphia!" "Wilmington!" And then, finally: "Baltimore!"

Jolting awake, I would gather my suitcase and my school-
bag—a lumpy peacock-blue shoulder bag stuffed not only
with my own books but with the many presents of books I
was always buying for Peter. We had met in a comparative
literature class the first semester of my freshman year; on one

24

of our first dates we had listened to recordings of Shakespeare at the library; and throughout our courtship, our conversation had been filled not only with our love for each other but with our mutual love of literature. Although we both knew that Peter was still too weak to read these books—such laughably "light" reading as the complete letters of Keats, the essays of Delmore Schwartz, an early novel by Henry James—they would be there to tempt him, as lures to get better.

Always at the end of my all-night journey, Peter's father would be there to greet me. With a silent nod, he would take my suitcase and whisk me away to visit my love, his son. It would have been nice had our destination been a fairy-tale castle, but instead we traveled in a limbo between hope and fear: during the long weeks of Peter's stay there, our first stop was the Johns Hopkins Hospital; later, it was the Baidas' apartment in suburban Baltimore, where Peter remained mostly bedridden during the debilitating ordeal of his radiation treatments.

Although the house in which I had grown up and where my parents still lived was no more than a ten-minute drive from Peter's, I preferred to keep these visits secret from my family. My reasons added yet another sad undertone to this season's music. My parents liked Peter personally, they assured me, but their distress was double: what would happen to Peter? they worried; but also what would happen to their daughter, if she continued her romance with someone whose medical future looked so unpromising?

My mother, whose empathy was such that she could not help but care for another mother's child, called Mrs. Baida periodically to check on Peter's progress and convey sincere concern. But knowing of her desire for me to break with Peter —"You can always be friends with him, Diane," she would tell me—I had come to the painful decision that I could not fight with my family and simultaneously keep my own spirit strong enough to help bolster Peter's as well. Instead, I stayed during these visits on a cot set up in Peter's room, next to his sickbed, so that we could hold hands across the

25

narrow space that separated us. This arrangement suited both Peter and me, but the secrecy also meant that I found myself growing inwardly distant from my family, and in particular from my mother, whose closeness I had always cherished.

Not being able to confide in Mom, the one person who had known all my moods (and who, I am sure in retrospect, in spite of our mutually agreed upon silence and in spite of my anger at her for challenging my romantic choice, still understood my turmoil better than I), left me adrift in an emotional isolation I could not have imagined. My other great confidant and intimate, of course, was Peter, to whom I also could not confess my greatest fears. It was as if I had lost my two anchors at once, and I was drifting, alone and confused, I knew not where.

Fortunately, by this time Peter's parents and I had begun forging close bonds of our own. During my frequent visits, Mrs. Baida and I would often sit at the kitchen table and pour out our feelings over a consoling cup of tea or coffee, using up what must have been cartons of Kleenex in the process and even occasionally finding reasons to laugh. The Baidas graciously extended to me the love and concern they so obviously felt for each other and for Peter, and before long Mrs. Baida had become Lil, and Mr. Baida, Erwin. Our single-minded goal was the same: to help Peter live.

Other close friends also helped build bridges not only to Peter but to me. One weekend, instead of the all-night train ride, I took an all-night car ride from Cambridge to Baltimore with Dick, Peter's best friend since junior high school, and Claudio, Peter's college roommate. Dick and Claudio alternated between driving and sleeping in the back seat, but throughout the long hours of the night, I remained in the front, talking nonstop in a hyperactive babble that did not fool anyone about just how worried I was. Gordon, another friend with whom Peter had grown up, was then in law school in Boston, and he would stop by periodically to treat me to dinner. Mike, whom I had known since junior high and who now lived on the same dormitory corridor, would knock on my door just to make sure depression hadn't gotten the better of me, as would so many other thoughtful friends and classmates.

But along with the comfort that these and many other old friends gave so generously, and that could be offered with unexpected empathy even by new acquaintances who had never met Peter, I also felt the anger and disappointment of discovering the limitations of others whom I had thought to be friends. In the journal I had begun keeping that semester, I find myself railing against a wide variety of insensitivities: There was the professor who had taught both Peter and me and who, though once more than cordial, suddenly became so uncomfortable in my presence that it was clearly painful for him even to nod hello. Then there was the high school friend just starting law school, who did not bother to respond to my January letter until the following August, saying, "Of course, I assume everything is fine by now; please write again soon."

Even now I read with amazement the journal entry citing an unnamed friend who felt it her "duty" to tell me, one evening, "There's no future in Peter. You should give him up." In a later entry, another friend shakes her head and says, "I couldn't do what you're doing; I just don't know how you do it." To her, I respond with equal candor, "But how could I *not* do what I'm doing?" Most devastating of all, there was Jill (as I shall call her), the dormitory neighbor and once close friend who responded to my concerns about Peter's health not with warmth but with a shocked silence so unmeltingly icy that from then on, whenever I even attempted to sit down at the same dormitory dining room table with her, she would abruptly rise, turn, and leave the room altogether.

In retrospect, I can begin to understand (even though I still cannot forgive) many of these actions as the reflex response of terror: Unschooled in the etiquette of grief, these acquaintances simply did not know how to respond to me, to Peter, or, most of all, to their own nagging and perhaps unconscious fear that, merely by associating with me, they might bring a similar fate on themselves or their families.

I understood that dread all too well because I shared it—an irrational but unshakable fear that I had traveled so far into the heart of this particular darkness that I had acquired a stigma, that the stigma would become contagious, that everyone who touched me would also become tainted, and that, finally, somehow my love for an ailing man would turn malignant and kill me, too.

Although I did not (or could not) articulate any of this, I developed a phobia, a displaced fear—a fear of flying, even at the same time that Erica Jong's novel of the same name was becoming a best-seller and a feminist rallying cry. My all-night train rides on "The Night Owl" were not only metaphorically resonant; they had become a psychological necessity.

In between those visits, I fell into other rhythms, heard other music, as well. Every night or two, I would place a long-distance call from Cambridge to Baltimore. In the first days and weeks that followed surgery, I thrilled to the sound of a voice growing stronger, fuller, finding new reserves of energy and spirit. He was getting used to his new face, Peter told me one night just after the bandages had come off; in fact, his new face was much better than he had expected: He could still smile with half his face, and half a smile was better than none. True, the right side of his face would always droop. The extensive scars down the side of his neck and chest were too thick, too red, ever to fade completely. Nor would the missing lower right earlobe and adjoining part of his jaw ever be completely masked, regardless of how full a beard Peter grew, was in fact starting to grow already. . . . There was a pause, in which I groped but found nothing to say. And then Peter said, "But it sure beats the alternative, doesn't it!" "Without a doubt!" I agreed, neither of us wishing or needing to say just how terrible the alternative was.

Then the radiation treatments began, and suddenly that grim alternative seemed far closer than we had thought.

Because the radiation treatments were focused on the side of Peter's face, we knew that his throat would be affected.

"So I'll have a sore throat," Peter joked. It was some sore throat. As the radiation treatments progressed, and the side effects accumulated and intensified, Peter was less and less able to eat, to speak, to swallow even liquids. Soon his diet consisted solely of liquid protein, painfully sipped through a straw. His hair fell out, first in small tufts, then in larger ones. He became so weak and skeletal that at one point, Peter, at five feet eight inches tall, weighed several pounds less than I, at five feet even. Unable to speak, in order to communicate at all Peter developed a simple sign language, or scrawled cryptic one- or two-line notes, and even these small efforts could exhaust him. When the radiation treatments were called off at last, it was because, as one of the doctors was overheard to comment, "We don't want to lose the patient."

To an outsider, my daily phone calls to Peter, an articulate young man whom illness had forced into muteness and fragility, may have seemed futile, even faintly absurd; but whenever I dialed the long-distance operator, it was always with the hope that this night's report might be better.

I can recreate those calls in memory: I had taken to studying each night in the large reading room of Widener Library, amid the endless rows of long, dark wooden tables. My idea was to force myself to spend time outside my narrow dormitory room and the terrible, enclosing isolation I had started to feel there. At the very least, the library's high ceilings would keep that claustrophobia at bay; at worst, I could always run into the downstairs ladies' room and weep silently in the stalls.

Next to the ladies' room was an old-fashioned telephone booth—the kind Clark Kent always used to change into Superman. How I wished that I could call upon his strength —better yet, turn into Supergirl herself. Instead, I dialed Peter's number, held my breath, and waited for Lil to answer and report what Peter was eating or not eating, what the doctor had said, what, if anything, Peter had managed to say. When she handed the receiver to Peter, I would hear a barely audible "Hello, Diane," and that would be my cue to begin my nightly nonstop patter—a mixture of concern for Peter, gossip, anecdotes, movie reviews, weather reports, literary critiques, current events commentary, and greetings from one and all. Sometimes I heard a faint cough, perhaps a laugh, occasionally a whole sentence, but usually no more than that. (Later, Peter revealed that he had saved up all his words for the day for those calls, even as I had saved all my cheerfulness for him.) After three or four minutes, he would say, "I love you, Diane." I would say, "I love you, Peter." And the connection would be broken until the next night.

Even as I write these words, I see myself emerging from that phone booth not as Supergirl but as a child who is shaken and weak, in need of a quiet place for solitude and tears. So I would step into the ladies' room, splash water on my bleary eyes, then return to the long rows of wooden desks upstairs. I would open my notebook, take out a pen, and begin writing. First a letter to Peter—a love letter, filled with chatter and tenderness, designed to cheer both of us up. And then, invariably, there would be a letter to myself, in the form of yet another entry in my journal.

I would stay at my chair until the library closed, writing, writing furiously, writing because that was the only thing that seemed to keep me sane. And as I wrote, I would sometimes remember a favorite play from high school, *Cyrano de Bergerac*. In it, Cyrano ghostwrites feverish love letters to the beautiful Roxanne on behalf of her handsome but empty-headed fiancé, until, one day, the tiny stain left by a teardrop reveals the depths of Cyrano's own love for Roxanne. My letters were of my own composition, but I sometimes wondered if Peter could see through the feigned cheerfulness with which I had filled them. Until I remembered: I had heard this same loving deception in the faintness of his voice: not just the sadness but the desperate hope, the lonely passion, and, finally, the tenderness—always the tenderness, always that.

And then, at the end of that season of letter writing, I copied and sent to Peter these lines from a sonnet by Shakespeare:

> *From you have I been absent in the spring,*
> *When proud-pied April, dressed in all his trim,*
> *Hath put a spirit of youth in everything,*
> *That heavy Saturn laughed and leaped with him.*
> *Yet nor the lays of birds, nor the sweet smell*
> *Of different flowers in odor and in hue,*
> *Could make me any summer's story tell,*
> *Or from their proud lap pluck them where they grew;*
> *Nor did I wonder at the lily's white,*
> *Nor praise the deep vermilion in the rose;*
> *They were but sweet, but figures of delight*
> *Drawn after you, you pattern of all those.*
> *Yet seemed it winter still, and, you away,*
> *As with your shadow I with these did play.*

The season of our absence from each other had actually been winter—a long, cold, bitter one. But by the time I wrote out those lines in the large, semilegible scrawl that Peter loved to mock, it was already May, and my choice contained not merely an acknowledgment of sadness but also a hint of hopeful expectation. The radiation treatments had ended, and Peter was tentatively planning a brief visit to Cambridge at the end of May. My college graduation was fast approaching, and now that those treatments really were in the past and Peter's recuperation could progress steadily, we were to be reunited at last. If we had any say in the matter, we swore in imitation of Shakespearean lovers, we would never be absent from each other in any season, ever again.

Perhaps a different spring was dawning, after all. I was preparing to move back to Baltimore, both to enter a graduate writing program at Johns Hopkins University that September and to be close to Peter while he regained his strength and we sorted out what came next. Although Peter was still too weak that summer to live independently—even "independently" with me to care for him—we began looking for an apartment to share in the fall, when Peter would resume his job teaching high school English at a private boys' school. As for what my parents would say to such a living arrangement —well, by then we might even be ready for that fight.

Meanwhile, now that the immediacy of illness and the urgent danger of the radiation treatments had passed, we not only had to learn to live in the same city and, later, in the same household, we also had to learn to live with doubt—with the unanswered question as to just how successful Peter's aggressive cancer treatment would prove.

There were also physical changes that required adjustments by both of us. "I must get used to you again" was the final line of a poem I wrote that summer. Those also were the words I had said to Peter the first time we attempted to make love after his operation. Throughout the long months, I had fought to keep my love for Peter whole and separate from his illness, but as we touched each other as lovers once again, there was not only the rediscovery of passion but the shocked realization of the extent to which his surgeon had redrawn his face, the degree to which the radiation treatments had ravaged his body. Even having regained his appetite and some of the weight he had lost, Peter remained shockingly thin—a fragile splinter of his former self. Gazing at Peter's smile— his new smile, with a slight lopsidedness that was accentuated by the new, frail thinness of his face—I knew that it would take time for me to survey the marks of illness along his face, neck, and chest with adoring eyes only, unmixed with pain. As yet, the scars were both literally and figuratively still too raw to the touch for me to trace them even with loving hands.

"I must get used to you again," I wrote. I would have to get used to Peter, but Peter would also have to get used to me, for though I had not changed in any visible sense, inwardly I felt different. The year of journeys had taught me to be physically self-sufficient and emotionally independent in many ways, but it had also taught me how much all of us depend on one another's care and love and even tolerance. In the end, I had become both more vulnerable and more steeled to life, and that change in me was like a new skin that could be tough or sensitive, seasoned or tender, and sometimes just as raw as Peter's scars.

It had not been easy. I had forced myself to find strength in the same way that Erwin had told me to find courage, by willing it into existence. I had needed all the reserves I could muster to make hard choices about Peter and my commitment to him, and in doing so I had learned more than I had bargained for not only about who I was but also about what the world was like, and about people at their best and worst.

But for the moment, all those reserves of strength, courage, and youthful blind optimism felt used up, depleted; or perhaps it was merely that the time had come to allow them to replenish themselves. Now I wanted to rest, to have fun, to learn to live again—to live not with doubt, but with Peter. To be in sync again, at last.

Sharing many of these feelings with me, Peter proposed that we take a new step on our mutual journey of restoration. We planned a trip, along with Peter's parents, to the beautiful Adirondack Mountains in upper New York State.

And then a curious gap appears in my journal. Even now, fifteen years later, I turn the page with an unbearable ache. For it was on that trip to the Adirondacks that I learned that my mother was dying, and suddenly I had no words—no words at all.

———

The archives of memory contain many haunting scenes, but for me my mother's dying remains the saddest—the one most filled with regret, and also, perhaps as a result, the one that has played and replayed itself through every subsequent loss.

There are so many scenes to recall. They all demand the closest scrutiny; they all present themselves in a jumble of words and images—the memory of her touch, the sound of her voice, the tangible feel of her presence, the tangible feel of her absence.

There I am, just hours before my trip to the Adirondacks,

leaning over to kiss Mom goodbye. She is lying in bed, trying to get over what she dismisses as some sort of viral bug. I am eager to believe her, for I'm anxious to go, cannot wait to go. Continuing our unspoken agreement, I leave no specific itinerary, and she demands none. There will be time enough for me to reveal all my secrets, for her to express all her concerns, when I return.

And then I am feeling a cool mountain breeze pour over me as Peter and I drive past the shimmering edge of Lake George, stop to tour the barricades at Fort Ticonderoga, and then return in a breathtaking haze of azure vistas to the quiet town of Tupper Lake, where Peter's aunt and uncle live and where our motel is located. Lil and Aunt Jenny have stayed behind at the house that day, and as we walk in the door, the first thing I see is Lil's eyes. They focus on me with sad intensity. "Diane, I'm going to tell you right away," she says. "Your mother was rushed to the hospital last night. Call your father."

After that, everything becomes a long-distance blur: "Your mother had an intestinal blockage," my father, playing what seems to be more the role of doctor than that of father, explains in his smooth Southern baritone. "She had an emergency colostomy. She'll be home in a few days."

"But what did the x-rays look like?" I insist, made both wise and bold by Peter's ordeal. "And what kind of a blockage was it? Was it a tumor? Was it malignant? What did the biopsy show?" But no matter what my question, my father stands by his line: "It was an intestinal blockage. We're not sure yet what it is."

Phrases meant to console can sometimes chill instead. Dad's carefully chosen words had been chosen too carefully. Or maybe I just knew my father too well, knew from years of dinnertime banter that not only he but all doctors are practiced in the arts of evasion. What is he evading now, I wonder, not just as a doctor but as a husband and father as well?

There is no time to consider, though, as I call the hospital directly. "Mom? Mom! It's me! It's Diane! How are you? How are you!" In the pause that follows, I imagine I see her face—weary, hopeful, despairing, all at once—and in a choked voice she tells me she's resting, she's feeling better. "Mom, don't cry, Mom," I say, knowing all too well why she is weeping at the sound of my voice. I know it is for the same reason that I am weeping at the sound of hers. It is because in the urgent, lonely worry of the hour when she was wheeled into the operating room, she must have thought that we would never speak again. But see, Mom? I say, like a six-year-old showing off her latest toy. See, here I am speaking to you, telling you I love you, I will be there beside you to care for you as soon as I can—care for you, as you have always cared for me. See? Everything will be all right. It must be.

And then I hang up the phone in a blur of tears that allows me to see nothing at all.

A day and a half later, as I enter the hospital room, the television is blaring in the background. Soon, its mélange of men's voices—Sam Dash, Sam Ervin, John Dean, John Ehrlichman, Bob Haldeman, and all the other players of the Watergate hearings—will become the endless background static to my daily visits here. But on this first visit, I pause for a moment to gaze at the middle-aged woman, dressed in her pink-flowered nightgown, covered in white bedsheets, and surrounded by baskets of yellow flowers. Her body is stout, while mine is thin, but her face is an older mirror of my own face, pale and furrowed, looking small and alone, watching the screen that hangs a foot in front of her. Then she looks up, her eyes suddenly brighten, and only when we break apart at last do I see the tubes, the machines, the IV bottles, and then the yellow-brown colostomy bag hanging above her.

Soon, we agree, she will go home to recuperate from her surgery, and that is the cheerful line we religiously adhere to on these visits in the middle of a sweltering Baltimore August. Our conversation is all evasive chitchat—what's in the mail, what's in the headlines, what weather will we have tomorrow. And then, one afternoon, Mom grasps my hand tightly and looks into my eyes. "Please promise me," she pleads. "Please, Diane. Promise me you'll never marry Peter."

I can feel the urgency of her touch, the coldness of my response. I open my mouth but say nothing. I cannot answer her. I cannot even look at her. I lower my eyes, loosen my hand, and turn away.

For so long, I have turned away, even in memory. I turned then, as I turn now, in anger and shame and guilt—at her, at myself. Yet my silence itself must have said all of this. It declared that I must have known even then that what Mom wanted most was to protect me, to shield me from pain or hurt of any kind—from Peter's illness and, no doubt, from her own. But she could not protect me. No mother ever can, no matter how hard or how earnestly she begs or pleads. I turned away because I could not tell her at that moment that she, like every parent, must fail in this, had failed already. I said nothing, nothing at all, because to say "No" out loud to her would have been to reject not only the illusion that she could shield me but also Mom herself and the safe haven of family home and family love she had struggled so fiercely to create for my brothers and me. Finally, to say "No" would mean that I, however much I wished, could not protect her, either—not from illness, not from my own choices.

Perhaps Mom knew all this, too, as she let my hand go. For as the months of her illness passed, she would never again make this request, nor even refer to this conversation. And during the course of those months, and after her death, and till the day I die, this unfinished conversation will remain unfinished—a symphony without a closing chord.

Denial, it has always seemed to me, is a way of knowing and not knowing at the same time—of wearing narrow blinders in order to avoid seeing what you nonetheless cannot help but see. At least, that is the particular version of denial that Mom and I seem to have acted out that year: We acknowledged and yet refused to acknowledge that this would be her last year. We conceded that fact yet also fought against it, each in her own way.

So did my entire family. It was while Mom was still in the hospital that I received a call from my brother Ronnie late one August morning to ask if he could he stop by to see me for a minute. Just one year older than I, Ronnie had always been the brother in whom I confided most easily. He was newly married, in his first year of law school, and holding down a full-time job. His schedule was full—too full for this visit to be casual. And so I sat on the front porch of the rambling old house I was sharing with a friend that summer (while Peter still recuperated at home) and waited for Ronnie to come and tell me news that I already knew, had known from the start: that our mother was dying.

Slowly, numbly, I wait. I rock back and forth, and then I see a familiar car pull over beneath the shade of a tall weeping willow. The car doors slam, and as first Ronnie, then his wife, Sharon, emerge, there is something in their very gait that declares their mission. When they come closer, I see that Ronnie's eyes, just a shade lighter than mine, are hazy and wet. I shake my head. "I know it's not good news," I say.

He nods. "Dad just told me. . . ."

Then we all go inside to call the surgeon directly, to ask our questions and hear the terrible details together: The tumor is malignant. The cancer has already spread to her lungs and liver. It is inoperable. Yes, she will come home from the hospital, but after that, it is only a matter of time. How much time is hard to say, though. She may have as little as three months to live. She may have several more. One never knows. One only knows that she is dying.

"Thank you," we say. What else do you say to a doctor who tells you your mother is dying?

Now we had the facts. But each of us in the family found ways to deny them, nonetheless. Sometimes this denial took the harmless form of little hopeful gestures of a gift or card or comment that suggested Mom would be with us, we would all be together, forever—resubscribing to a complete chamber music concert series for the following season, for instance, or going shopping for a new red raincoat for the next spring.

Another gift commemorated the central role she had played in our lives and that we had played in hers. On her final birthday, we gave her a ring containing the birthstones of her three children and two daughters-in-law, which she could wear and enjoy. And in fact, these acts of hope and love turned out to be far more than wishful thinking, for Mom, spurred on by hopes and desires of her own, lived to attend almost every performance in that concert series. And seeing in that ring reasons both to have lived and to continue to live, Mom wore it proudly every day until her death.

But there were other times when we would just avoid her eyes—even to look at her could be too painful a reminder that one day, soon, that sad, comforting gaze would not be there at all. Games of avoidance could go even further. In the course of the months that followed, each of my two brothers, my father, and I separately found an excuse to escape for a small vacation, if only a weekend vacation—an escape from the daily confrontation with what was happening, another form of denial. At the same time, my father would contend throughout Mom's illness, and for years later, that "Mum never knew that she was dying, not until the very end."

But Mom did know. She had wanted to know, had needed to know, and I had been the one to tell her.

This was the terrible task for which, in my innocence, she had prepared me years before. She had often told me the story of how, after our next-door neighbor, Dr. M., had discovered his wife was dying, he had thrown the confirming x-rays in the wastebasket and told his wife that she was fine, fine, nothing to worry about. But Mrs. M. had been trained as a nurse and still worked part-time in her husband's office. One day, at work, she had found her x-rays in the wastebasket, read them, and discovered the truth for herself.

"And that's how she was able to do what she had to do that year," Mom had told me many times through the years. "She was able to write her will and put all her papers in order. It gave her the chance to do all of that. If it were me—when it is me—I want to be able to do that, too."

Remembering that story—unable, in that terrible summer, to forget that story—I knew, or thought I knew, that when the time came, Mom would want to know, too: would want to have that final chance to put her papers in order, put her life in order. And so I waited for her surgeon to tell her. For Dad to tell her. For my brothers to tell her. But no one told her, was willing to tell her, could bear to tell her. In this way, she recuperated from her operation and left the hospital, uncertain about her prognosis but glad to be returning home.

By the time she stepped inside her front door for the first time since that emergency ride to the hospital several weeks before, it was the end of August. Nixon had resigned, had gone home to California, even as Mom was going home, to the house where she had reared her three children. The Jewish New Year was just around the corner—a new year that was bringing so many things for her to look forward to: My oldest brother, Jeffrey, was entering his final year of medical school and would receive his degree at the end of that year. I, her third and youngest child, would be receiving my master's degree that same spring. And just the year after that, Ronnie would get his degree from law school. All her children were about to launch themselves into the world; two were married already, and as for me, the third—well, there were worries, but even so, there was much to look forward to.

This was her mood that late August afternoon when the two of us sat chatting in her bedroom at home and the subject of the future—not her children's, but her own—came up at last.

I remember that scene, and I am there once again: We are talking, talking idly about a future that I cannot bear to think about because she will not be there to share it. And suddenly, I cannot bear the charade anymore. "But, Mom—oh, Mom, it's cancer," I blurt out. And I tell her. I see her wide, despairing, questioning gaze.

"How long?" she asks, with the stunned look of a boxer who has taken the punch of a lifetime.

"I don't know—a year, more or less." I give more time than

the surgeon does, but however much time I give, it would not be enough.

"A year, more or less," she repeats.

I purse my lips to hold back tears. I have the terrible urge to run far, far away and never return. Oh, Mom! I want to cry out. I'm just doing what you asked me to do, over and over, through the years! But now that I'm telling you, am I being your helper, am I doing what you really want? "Mom, I'm sorry—I—" But I cannot even begin to enumerate all the many things that I am sorry about at that moment. I look at her, her downcast face, too shaken even for tears, and then, still a child—her child—I do run away. Abruptly, I stand and leave the room. To my shame, I leave her alone. Because I must be alone, away from this unbearable scene. I leave her because I cannot face her. I cannot face her because I cannot bear to lose her.

I no longer remember where I go, but later that afternoon, I return. I want to apologize, take back the words, take back the scene, take back time itself. But neither of us says a word. It is as if this scene has never happened. Except for this: Already, Mom has begun to do just what her next-door neighbor did, years before. Already she has called her lawyer to set up an appointment to discuss her will. Will I accompany her to the bank next week to look over some things with her there?

It is extraordinary to remember the numb turmoil, the calm inner terror, the careful steps with which we managed to go through all those paces that fall: of banking and lawyering, but also shopping and housekeeping and gossiping and all the other daily business of life, of both our lives. Life goes on in spite of everything, even when life is ending.

It went on, even as Mom and I sat together on that final Jewish New Year and heard the cantor intone the holiday's central prayer: "Who shall live? Who shall die? On Rosh Hashanah it is written, on the solemn fast of Yom Kippur it is sealed." We recite this prayer, as if there might be a second opinion, God's opinion, to counter the doctor's decree.

But prayer itself is a form of hope, and so we pray, almost desperately, that in spite of what the doctors say, the Great Book of Life has not yet closed for Mom. And suddenly we believe, as we cry out that prayer with all the fervor in our hearts, that it is just as Jewish tradition says: that the volume that records our fate is not yet sealed. Pray long enough and hard enough, and perhaps there will still be time—time, after all. . . .

Nonetheless, when we return home from the synagogue, I take out my camera and insist on snapping photographs. I demand family photographs, but already it is a modified family, dispersed. My oldest brother, Jeffrey, and his wife, Linda, were not able to get away from Philadelphia, where Jeffrey is finishing medical school, to come to Baltimore for this particular holiday. Ronnie's wife, Sharon, is with her family. My father, always the workaholic, has returned to his office. And so Geraldine, our housekeeper, tells us to to say "Cheese" as Mom, Ronnie, and I stand all in a row, smiling at the camera as if nothing is different on this holiday from any other in the past. We stand outside, and the late-afternoon sun makes us all squint—even Mom, in spite of the fact that she is wearing one of her favorite hats, a white hat with a long, thin feather that reminds me of Robin Hood. The hat casts a slight shadow across her face, even as she and I link arms and stare into the camera.

The camera clicks; the moment is caught forever. And now, as I look at those pictures years later, I want to rush back in time, jump into the photograph and say to my younger self: "Diane! Don't look at the camera, look into your mother's face! Capture her expression not just on film but in your memory! Kiss her, hug her, move closer!"

There are so many happy-painful moments, so many poignant moments, so many partly painful moments, so many purely painful moments in that year of pain. If I could, I would recapture, rewrite, rearrange all these instants when we touch but do not quite touch. And I would speak out loud, at last, the many words left unsaid between us—words I wish that I, she, both of us, had risked: words about love and caring and, finally, about Peter—about my love for him and about my anger at this silence, at not being able to share my happiness with her, the one other person in the world I loved so deeply and the one whose own happiness I cared for most.

But whenever one of us would begin to risk those words, the other would choose silence. And somehow all our scenes followed a script of their own, as on the afternoon when Mom said to me, "Sit down, I want to talk to you. I've been thinking about something." I was in a rush to get to class—a class that I can no longer recall and that even then I did not much care about. But then, I was always in an unbearable rush that year —unbearably afraid of what I might hear, afraid of what I might not hear; afraid of what I might say, afraid of what I might not say.

And so I rushed away from her, and then rushed back again. But already it was too late. It always was. When I returned, later that afternoon, it was Mom who no longer wished to speak. Now it was I who wanted to speak of love and care and continuing to care, and it was she who held out her hands to stop me: "Don't say it, Diane. Please don't say anything, because then you'll cry, and if you cry, I'll cry too."

And so we said nothing, revealing everything, as we had before, as we would again.

———

From Peter's bout with illness I had learned lessons about courage and strength and perspective—or so I thought. But now that it came time to face the medical facts—that however much I prayed or hoped or deceived myself otherwise, this would be my mother's final illness—those lessons seemed like useless abstractions, a textbook from another life.

I had grown weak from so much grief in so short a span of time. I did not want to apply all those sad lessons once again. I did not want to learn any more lessons at all. But life went on, and loss went on, and the lessons went on.

I learned, in spite of myself, that suffering is a beast that each of us must fight on his or her own terms. The way Mom chose to endure her ending would be—must be—different from the stoical way Peter had coped with uncertainty mixed with hope. But in spite of these differences, all of us used silence, each in his own way, to deny, to deceive, and, finally, to keep faith: Peter's silence reflected his deep fatalism, while Mom's acted as a shield of dignity. And for all of us, silence was a mask that concealed our fear—a disguise that ultimately proved both an ally and an enemy.

I also saw that when tragedy strikes, some families close ranks and grow stronger, as Peter's had. But others separate and weaken, even as mine did that year. For my family's silence had not merely masked fear, it had bred isolation, until not only Mom and I, but Jeffrey, Ronnie, and Dad, all of us, were living under unspoken rules of silence. Mom was the force that had kept us together as a family. Now, as she faded, I felt our family, too, was dying. Soon, without her, silence itself would lose its meaning. Would we ever connect again? Would the death of my mother be the death of my family as well?

In less than a year, I thus found myself playing two different roles in two different families, two different dramas. But how could I—how could anyone—be expected to keep such divergent, conflicting scripts straight? Here I was playing out my roles of devoted young lover one moment and devoted young daughter the next—roles that, given the circumstances, could not help but create internal struggles, conflicts, and tensions that tore at me relentlessly through my season of grief.

This anguished subplot in a year of plots is most concretely dramatized by the black vinyl-covered pocket calendar on which I recorded the daily struggle to find time to balance all these diverse emotional demands.

Look at that year's calendar and you will see the ruptured rhythm of hours, days, nights, split between lives: On Wednesday night, I go to the concert with Peter and his family; on the next night, I go to the opera with Mom. The next night, a Friday, is, as always, reserved for dinner with Mom and Dad; while Saturday night, as always, is for Peter. Sunday brunch is optional—sometimes with Peter, sometimes with Mom.

Now turn the page, and the week begins again: I wake early each morning and see Peter off to his teaching job, then begin all my many tasks not only as lover and daughter but as graduate student and aspiring writer. I sit at my desk for two hours to compose my graduate thesis, then take a break at ten, when Mom calls to say good morning, what's my schedule for the day? I know it as well as she does. At noon, I will put down my pen and get in my car. I will stop at the deli or grocery store to pick up some luncheon treats to tempt her—tempt both of us—to eat. We will nibble on sandwiches and sip tea, and then I'll be off again, to yet another world: my life as a graduate student at Johns Hopkins University. And as I ride through the dappled, tree-lined streets of Baltimore, these drives become my daylight equivalents of last year's rides on "The Night Owl"—surreal journeys between the world of the living and the world of the deathly ill.

When I finish with class, I will return to the apartment that I share with Peter, where I will devote an hour alone to sadness and fatigue. I will lie on my bed, cup my face in my hands, and cry. Perhaps I will open my journal to rail at this terrible year. And then I will hear Peter's key in the door as he returns from work; or perhaps the phone will ring—it's Mom again, just calling to say hello, did I know a ballet would be on TV that night? And so I dry my eyes, and the cycle begins again. . . .

My strategy is to fill every available moment in advance: I begin writing free-lance book reviews for the *Baltimore Sun*; I take on a nonpaying job as "women's editor" of a small local newspaper called *City Dweller*. And I begin jogging at a high school track each morning with an old friend. Ostensibly, the free-lance writing and editing will give me credentials for my résumé, so I can hunt for a paying job when I graduate. Ostensibly, the jogging is to help keep me in shape in a city dominated by cars. But really, the idea is to work like hell, to crowd as many waking minutes as possible with so much fuss and bustle that I can no longer think, no longer worry, no longer care. Most of all, I will have no time to look back—look back and see what awful thing is gaining on me. I am, quite literally, running for my life.

I am also—sometimes admittedly, sometimes not—running from reality: the knowledge that soon I will be a motherless child. More than that, a motherless child who has had to deny her mother a dying wish.

And so I run, I work, I dash from one activity to another in order to escape, to be somebody, anybody, other than a terrified daughter or lover—to be a book reviewer, an editor, an anonymous graduate student. And then something strange and scary and seductively comforting begins to happen: I actually begin to imagine that I might escape. I will just disappear one day and never return. I will walk out of my life and never come back, just like that. Why, if Jack Nicholson had dared to do it in Antonioni's new movie, *The Passenger*—a film I go to see several times in hypnotic fascination—why, oh, why, couldn't I?

Of such stuff are fantasies and obsessions made. One morning, as the early songbirds of spring are chirping outside my window, these fantasies capture me in a particularly vivid way. Along with the songbirds, I become convinced I hear a woman's voice calling me. It is soft and high—my mother's voice, but as if from another world. I shudder, even as I listen, in a vain attempt to understand these soft and soothing syllables that have no meaning.

I listen some more, and I remember Virginia Woolf, whose life and work I had studied in college. Virginia Woolf was only twelve when her mother died, and the echoes of that early loss resonated throughout her life. She, too, had suffered periods of fantasy and depression. And one morning, she had heard the birds speak to her in Greek. . . .

This language was not yet Greek, but I knew then, at last, that I had run quite far enough. I also knew that I could never run hard enough or fast enough to outdistance grief. It had overtaken me at last, and I must yield to it. I did not even need to look back to see it gaining on me; the familiar beast was there beside me, smiling its terrible sweet smile.

Giving in—admitting defeat even after the most contentious race—can come as a relief. Perhaps, I realized then, I did not need to be strong, after all. In fact, I could not be strong any longer. And in my weakness, I began to cry. So this is the breaking point, I thought: My strength is broken. I am broken. And soon, without Mom, my whole world will be broken, too.

Then, when I had finished crying, I picked up the phone and called the university health services, arranged to see a psychologist, and prepared to weep and rage, as selfishly and angrily as any child: No, she cannot leave me—not now, not now, not now.

———

It has often struck me that in many ways Mom willed herself to stay alive that year. When the tumor was discovered in early August, the doctors—including my father—had given her no more than one season to live. But she remained vital through that summer, autumn, and winter, and it was only as spring broke that she began to lose her strength noticeably and fail. But she still had promises to keep, and having come so close to meeting them, she refused to give in: On Sunday, May 18, Jeffrey graduated from medical school in Philadelphia. Later that same week, on Friday, May 23, I graduated from my master's program at Johns Hopkins. And Mom, by now in a wheelchair, attended both ceremonies, proudly hugged her children and celebrated with the family she had held together for a quarter of a century. Having done all that, she retired to her bed at home and did not leave the house again. She died on the afternoon of Monday, June 9, 1975. She was fifty-eight years old.

Her death came one day after Ronnie and Sharon's first wedding anniversary; she had called to wish them happiness.

And so she had seen all her children launched and settled. In the weeks and months before, she had also, to the best of her ability, arranged for the care of her aged parents and her reclusive sister in Cleveland. She had done what she wanted that year, and she had died in dignity, in her own bed at home. She was not an unfinished woman, and she had not led an unfinished life.

When it came, she was ready for the end. I am convinced of that and grateful for it. But though we knew the end was near, we also refused to know and were not prepared. For the living, death always comes as a shock, no matter how long or certain the knowledge that what is coming will come.

I had spent the day before playing the piano for Mom. I serenaded her as I had through all the years of my growing up: Bach, Mozart, Schubert, Beethoven. The music would comfort her, I hoped. At the very least, she would know I was nearby. All afternoon long, I would play a sonata or an opera tune, then run upstairs to Mom's bedside and ask eagerly, "Did you hear that? Did you recognize that? You used to love to hear me play that. You used to play that yourself. Should I play Brahms now? Would you like that? Would you?" She would nod, and I would run downstairs again and play again. And in the music, I prayed, I would say everything that needed to be said, and she would hear it.

The music was my way of saying goodbye to her. I could not actually say the word "goodbye." I could not allow myself to know that this was actually "goodbye," even though Geraldine had asked me, "Did you say goodbye to her?" I could not say the word, even though the nurse who had been hired to watch over Mom those last few days had shown me her stethoscope and said, "I'm ready."

I knew and refused to know. Early on the day of my mother's death, I went over to visit Mom, to play the piano some more, and Geraldine had asked me, "Did you do everything your mother asked you to do?" Taking the question all too literally, I remembered that Mom had asked me, some time before, to buy a briefcase for Ronnie as a law school gradua-

47

tion present. With mad determination, I went to the local shopping center and picked one out for him, returned home once more, and whispered to Mom, "I did what you wanted, Mom. I love you, Mom. I'll be back soon, Mom."

And then, feeling an emotional exhaustion wash over me, I left Mom with Geraldine and the nurse, and drove the short distance to the apartment Peter and I shared, where I lay down on my bed and wept. It must have been a little after two in the afternoon, for a few minutes later, Peter arrived home from teaching and, seeing me in tears, began to comfort me. Then the phone rang, and it was the rabbi. "Diane, your mother just died. I'm sorry," he said.

"So soon?" I said. "So suddenly?"

"But I thought you knew . . ." he said, startled.

It was just before three o'clock. And I had known and refused to know, all along.

Two days later, after the rabbi had delivered the funeral sermon and the reddish dirt had been thrown on my mother's grave; and after we had returned to the house to which she would never return again, I wandered through the rooms and listened for the sound of her presence. The house was filled with grieving friends and relatives, with all the sounds of sadness, and with all the signs of mourning. Already, my brothers and father and I had donned old, black clothes to sit *shivah*, the traditional seven days of mourning. At the funeral home, the rabbi had pinned black crepe sprigs on our lapels and slashed them with a razor blade—symbols of the mourner's rent clothes. We were to wear the slashed sprigs all seven days. We had covered all the mirrors with white sheets, so the evil eye would not cast a spell on us; really, I think, so we would not see our own ghostly faces. I wandered from room to room and accepted the embrace of now one relative and now another, and each room was filled with sympathy and warmth. Perhaps, later on, I would be able to hear these voices again in memory, and they would comfort me. But for the moment, the house was empty, and the voices did not register. The house was empty of her, and it would never be full again.

Still later, after the guests had left and my father, my brothers, and I were left alone, each with a separate grief, I felt the minutes stretch into hours—new hours, unlike any I had lived before, without the life that had given me life. I was a child again, but this time a motherless child. Was this what it felt like to breathe? To eat? To sleep? To wander through the world in search of someone I had lost and could not find again?

It would be many days, weeks, and months before I could begin to see that Mom was still in that house and would always be there, but transformed into the various legacies of love and care and spirit and will that she had so carefully worked to leave behind for all of us that year.

I saw the first glimmer of that legacy in the unexpected notes Mom had left me—little scraps, stuck in a drawer or cabinet, on which Mom had scrawled, "These things belong to Diane." They were there to alert me, as in a will, to the engraved silver tea set or the set of Quimper dishes that she wanted me to have, as remembrances of her.

I cried out in pain and wonder at each discovery. This was in the days immediately following the *shivah*, as I went through and cleaned the house with Geraldine, Mom's confidante those last weeks and months. Without Mom, the house had become a haunted house; her presence was there, her new red raincoat hung in the closet, and all the beautiful Delft antique plates and Spode figurines she had saved up money to collect through the years still stood in place on the knickknack shelves where she had arranged them. Everything was in place, just as she had left it. But she herself was not there, would never be there again. And now it was my job to remove the raincoat from the closet, to fold up the dresses, to take the gloves and scarves and slips and nightgowns from the dresser drawers, and to fold them neatly away in a box, for someone else to take away.

Opening each closet door, I felt as if I were violating my

mother's final dignity, her privacy, and that I would learn some terrible secret no daughter should ever know. That secret was worse than any curse. It was reality: My mother was dead. She would never need any of these things again.

But now, as we went through her dresses, hats, and coats to put them away, forever, Geraldine's presence beside me was also like a gift from Mom. For as we worked together, sorting through Mom's pastel-pink and yellow scarves, or gazing for the last time on her favorite blue-and-white polka-dot sundress or the exotic white-tasseled turban she had worn to my brother's bar mitzvah, Geraldine could tell me all the things that Mom had told her those last months—all the things that, in fact, Mom had not been able to tell me but had instructed Geraldine to say on her behalf: to tell me, first, that Mom had known all along that Peter and I had been living together that year. "Your mother knew that everything you did was out of respect for her," Geraldine told me, and that was true. Our silence, I now saw, was not simply denying or refusing to know the truth; it was also acknowledging the truth in a different way. For in addition to everything else, it had been out of respect for Mom that I had not wished to burden her with a living arrangement I knew would trouble her. And it was out of her respect for me that Mom had not wished to burden me further with requests or demands she knew I would not be able to meet. Through our silence, it seemed, we had simply agreed to disagree, in mutual love and deference.

As we sorted through the piles of papers, letters, cards, pictures, programs, and many other keepsakes Mom had saved through the years, I also found another gift—the gift of memory, or, as Proust might have said, the gift of recaptured time. From the grocery bills and laundry lists, I could reconstruct the daily details of her life. More than that, the snapshots, report cards, holiday greeting cards and letters amassed through the years recorded the growth of all of us as a family. Most poignant of all, at the very top of a box filled with such mementoes, I found a postcard of a painting by

Matisse, a domestic scene all bright purple and fuchsia, that I had given Mom just the month before, for what would prove to be her last Mother's Day. "Dearest Mom," I wrote. "This picture captures the warm spirit, harmony, and love that you have always brought to our house. All my love, Diane." The accompanying gift was a gold-plated pin of a Scythian griffin, a mythical symbol of guardian protection. Mom made sure to wear it at my graduation; you can see it in all the photographs we took that day, the last pictures of her we have.

What came through most strongly not only in this card but in all the different notes and cards and tokens through the years was that though this last year had seemed to be filled with silence, the words had not been left unsaid. They had been said many times, repeated over and over without our even knowing it. Or perhaps Mom had known it, all along. Now I knew it, too.

But that was only one small stage of a journey whose length I could not foresee. In the same way that I had said to Peter, "I must get used to you again," I now had to get used to the terrible void left by my mother's death. The feeling was so new, so raw, that though I could sort through the different objects in my mother's house, at first, and for a long time, I could not bring myself to use the dishes, the scarves, the silver that belonged to her—to her, and not to me. I could not accept them as gifts to me, nor could I yet give to my brothers and their wives the various objects that Mom had wanted them to have. For months, all these boxes sat untouched in an attic room at the top of the house—a haunted room at the top of a haunted house, yearning for the ghost that had given it life as Heathcliff yearned to be haunted by Cathy in *Wuthering Heights*. I could not even discard the boxes of clothes that Geraldine and I had so carefully packed away. I left to my father the task of actually calling Goodwill—a task that he put off for months, as no doubt I would have done as well.

Before I was able to unlock that attic door, I needed time to unlock the pain and hurt I felt within. For when I had closed the door behind me on my mother's house, I could not escape the feeling that I had lost my home, my sense of place, forever.

Instead, I was adrift—lost and abandoned, unmoored. I was free to escape at last, but now all I wanted was to recover what I had lost.

I attempted to do so in two ways—first, through an actual journey; then, through a journey of the imagination.

The actual journey was a trip to Cleveland, my mother's home town, in search of her past. In a sense, I went on behalf of my mother as well as myself. My grandparents, her parents, were now senile, uncomprehending of the world. Through the year of her illness, they had grown both frailer in health and more detached from reality. Now my grandparents and their reclusive daughter, my aunt, lived in their big sad house in Shaker Heights, cared for by nurses and overseen by my grandmother's younger brother (himself in his seventies) and his wife.

Throughout Mom's year of illness, that household's future had weighed heavily on her mind. In spite of her own failing strength, she had visited several times to do what she could to assure continuity after her death. Each time she had returned sadder than before, but when I had offered to accompany her, she had declined: "Remember them as they were, Diane. It so breaks my heart to see them now, I can hardly bear to go myself."

As soon as I entered the front door on the trip after my mother's death, I knew why. "I'm Diane," I tell my grandparents, as they respond to my hugs as to the kindness of a friendly stranger. "Diane," I repeat. "Diane—Roselda's daughter—" and I point to one of the many pictures of my brothers and me that sit atop the black Knabe upright piano.

"Oh, Roselda? You wanted to see Roselda?" my grandmother asks, smiling now. "Roselda's away at school."

My grandfather nods, wearing the same broad grin he had cheerfully bestowed upon his grandchildren through all the years of our growing up. But now the grin is hollow, set. "Who is your mother?" he asks, in the same gracious, slightly flirtatious style that I remember from my childhood. "You're such a nice girl, your mother must be a nice woman, too."

I smile, nod, look around, but my aunt is not there. She is in another room, alone, not wishing to see the visitor from out of town. And so I feel lost here—as lost as my mother must have felt on those last visits home. For there was no longer a home for her to go to, as now there is no home for me.

But there is also some healing, as I visit with the many first, second, and third cousins of this large, once close family, and I hear stories and see pictures from decades ago: Mom going to a college dance and staying out all night long . . . Mom putting her hands to her mouth as she gossips with her girlfriends over tea . . . Mom excitedly announcing her engagement to be married . . . And these images of a woman who loved life help blur those last pathetic images of a woman so weak she cannot lift her hand to eat, a woman so frail she can barely grasp my hand and, in letting go of that grasp, lets go of her role as the strong, loving mother who had cared for me all my life.

Most resonant of all these recaptured images is the glimpse I have of my parents' wedding, twenty-seven years before. I relive that moment in my second journey—my journey of the imagination—which occurs when I attend services at the synagogue where their wedding took place. It is Saturday morning, and as the Sabbath service progresses, I sit alone, off to the side. I gaze at the sanctuary's Tudor wood paneling, the marble pulpit, the cool, high ceiling. Then I look at the rabbi and the cantor standing there in their black robes and wonder, Can they be the very same rabbi and cantor who performed my parents' wedding so many years ago?

They are—I recognize them from the pictures in my parents' wedding album. And as the cantor chants the morning service, other pictures come alive in memory: Yes, there my mother walked in her ivory gown. There her train flowed behind her, there her shoes touched the hardwood floor, there, perhaps, a splinter caught the lace of her hem. The silk train shone in the soft light of the summer evening, and she could not hold back her tears.

Now the service continues, and to hold back my own tears, I force myself to listen to the rabbi's commentary on that morning's reading from the Torah and the Prophets. This is the first of the seven Sabbaths of Consolation, he tells us. These Sabbaths fall immediately after the solemn Fast of Av, which commemorates the destruction of the Temple, and the readings are meant to comfort us even as we mourn. And then he begins to chant the verses from Isaiah:

> *Comfort ye, comfort ye My people,*
> *Saith your God.*
> *Bid Jerusalem take heart,*
> *And proclaim unto her*
> *That her time of service is accomplished,*
> *That her guilt is paid off;*
> *That she hath received of the Lord's hand*
> *Double for all her sins.*

As the verses continued, suddenly, for the first time I was comforted. And when my trip had ended, I knew what I must do. I knew that I must remake my life—make a new life, with a new job, and in a new city. I would begin again, as I had begun again after Peter's illness, only to be crushed by the long agony of my mother's dying.

———

I needed to create a new life, but I also needed to recover my old one. For throughout that year and a half, there had never been time to recover and reclaim those parts of me that had been battered and lost. Now it was time to heal and, if not to escape, at least to move on.

Certainly, one of the tasks before me—that of making an independent life for myself—was a task faced by any young adult entering the world on her own. Like most adolescents, all through college I had railed against the sheltering protection of my parents—a conflict all too vividly dramatized by my mother's desire to shield me from Peter's illness. But it is one thing to recklessly renounce, escape, or steal away from the safe haven of home knowing it will be there when the prodigal returns. It is quite another to turn away knowing that if you try to return, you will face only a house filled with ghosts.

Now I turned, and I saw that the events of my out-of-sync life had left me so many haunted images and memories that I must escape. Even as Mom had grown weaker that year, Peter had gradually regained his strength, until their faces seemed oddly like mirrors moving in opposite directions. At the same time, the closer Mom approached her end, the more she had resisted talking about it. Now that Peter was recovering, however, his silence suddenly turned into unrelenting conversation about and meditation on his own brush with death. But that meant that wherever I turned—whether to Mom, or to Peter—there would always be some reminder, visual or verbal, of the reality of loss.

I understood Peter's need. Peter, like me, is a writer, but it is not only writers who need words to make sense of life. There is something about telling a tale again and again that in and of itself gives shape and meaning to experience. Psychotherapy is one such form of catharsis. Writing is another. In retrospect, I see that I had begun keeping a journal at the start of Peter's illness for just that reason: If I could tame my life on paper, I thought, surely I could tame it in reality. This need breeds a tone of quiet, desperate yearning, and so familiar did I become with that tone that even now, when I pick up someone's memoir to read, I can sense from the very first lines when a personal history is not just a memory but a memorial, written to recapture in words or perhaps to discover for the first time the purpose, sense, or context of a life.

That fall, Peter had started writing a memoir of his illness as a way of trying to understand what it had meant to him. He called his memoir "Living in Doubt." But the act of writing was also, in its way, Peter's own method of confronting the undertow of doubt and uncertainty that cancer implied. Once he had been able to articulate his fears, perhaps he would be able to live not *in* doubt but *with* it, as with an old, familiar, if not always welcome friend, whose presence could come to be accepted and even, sometimes, forgotten.

To help him reconstruct that time, Peter often asked me to return in memory with him to the days and weeks of his illness—to describe to him how I had felt, to analyze my feelings, to discover how our perspectives had been both similar and different. He had saved all the letters I wrote that year, and as a further aid to his research, I gave him my pocket calendar and journals—gifts that spurred additional discussion about love and loss.

This is how it came about that I would return exhausted from a visit to my mother, who was dying, and spend the evening with a lover who was preoccupied with staying the ghosts of death. Often Peter would try to comfort me, but he still needed comforting himself, and for the moment our ideas of what comfort meant were perhaps inevitably askew.

No wonder that after a time, so much fraught silence, heaped upon so many painful memories, began to weigh oppressively on me. That burden grew and grew, until even Peter's touch seemed like a burden I could no longer support. Sadly, we decided to part for a time. We would sort things out alone, to see if we could find a way to bring not just comfort, love, and caring to each other, but hope as well.

I decided to move to Washington, a city that, at just forty miles and an hour's ride away from Baltimore, was close enough to Peter and to my family to remain in easy contact, but far enough to allow me to heal at a pace my own heart set. I hoped to find an editorial position in Washington, while Peter planned to resume his teaching job that fall. In that period of separation, something important happened. We began courting all over again on our weekend commutes, and, unaware, we fell in love all over again. Eventually, we found an apartment together and committed ourselves to each other as devotedly as we had before. But without that period of grace in which to mourn, I'm not so sure we would have found so happy an ending to our troubled year.

My studio apartment near Washington's Dupont Circle provided the independence—the "escape" from other people's needs—that I had wanted. By learning to live alone, I was preparing myself for—and steeling myself against—the possibility of a world in which I would be bereft of everybody, by which I meant the two people in the world about whom I cared most. With Peter's illness, and then Mom's death, I had got used to one form of darkness. That darkness had engulfed me in sadness, until I, too, needed to learn to hope again.

But even as I forced myself to learn to live alone, without my mother's presence in the world, in fantasy and dreams I still could not accept the fact of her death. The phone would ring, and I would run to pick it up. Mom had always found a way to call; she had even sent a message through the notes she had left me after her death. Irrationally, and yet yearningly, I wondered, could it be her now? Or perhaps, I would tell myself as I drowsed in the half-dreamy state of early morning, if only I could find the right exchange, I would be able to call her. I would tell her all the news I had been storing up for her, that I so longed to tell her: That I had found a good job and was getting along all right. And I would also tell her that Peter and I were working things through, that we were together again, and I would hear her say she was happy to know that, too, because after all, this was what she wanted for her daughter—someone who would care for her.

In that early-morning dream state, my mind would wander more, and I would not only hear my mother's voice, I would see her face. Oh, it had all been some terrible mistake, she would tell me—it wasn't she who was buried beneath the reddish dirt, it was someone else. She herself had been alive all the time, and here she was beside me, reaching out to touch me, assure me, comfort me. Her outstretched arms would come closer, closer still, would reach out to encompass me once more. . . .

And then the alarm clock would go off, and I would be left with the terrible knowledge that the phone had not rung, would never ring. I would rub my eyes against the harsh glare of the morning light and know that however far I stretched and reached, only in my dreams would I ever feel that comforting embrace again.

I would never find her, however far I searched or wandered. Nonetheless, that fall I got into the habit of stopping off at the National Gallery of Art each evening after work and revisiting the many galleries through which I had used to ramble with my mother on our periodic visits to Washington. The museum's late hours—until nine most evenings except in winter—allowed me to make close studies, in particular, of the dark, late self-portraits of Rembrandt and of the only painting by Leonardo in the United States, the haunting Ginevra de Benci. And as I stared into the soft brown eyes of the melancholic young matron of Florence, and then into the fierce sadness of Rembrandt's, I thought my own eyes looked back at me.

When winter came, the museum's hours shortened, and at work each day, I would wear one of the pastel-colored silk scarves that Mom had worn, and feel its warmth. In the evenings, I took up reading poetry and began to write a memoir of my mother's life. Dreams had helped, and getting the facts down on paper would be yet another way of recovering and preserving her presence.

Then spring came around again, and suddenly I realized how much I had missed playing the piano in the past year. I had hardly played since I had last played for Mom, and though the reason I gave was that my apartment was too small for a piano, in truth I had no heart to play for myself or for anyone else. But now, as the first anniversary of her death approached, it occurred to me that playing music would be a way of playing for her—for us both. In the same way that I had said goodbye to her through music on that last afternoon, I would be able to keep her memory alive.

With this in mind, I impulsively stepped inside a music

store one sultry spring day after work and bought a used silver flute for a little under one hundred dollars. I had never played the flute, and I knew no teacher in town. But the pure, bright sound had always attracted me, and the price tag in the window was right. I paid in cash and told myself: This is Mom's present to me; not just the flute, but the music itself.

That summer, even as I learned to play the flute, I learned to live again, came alive again. I would play a new instrument, and more than that, I would live my life in a new key, with a new and different tone. I had changed, and Peter had changed, and the bond between us had also changed—grown tenderer and tougher. It was in the same month I bought my flute that we found an apartment and began living together again.

I had healed alone and now we could heal together. I remembered my words to Peter at the time of his illness: "I must get used to you again." This time, I had needed to get used to myself; I had needed to create a new self.

Just rehearse one slow note after another, I told myself, and listen carefully. For it was all like learning to play the flute. It was all like learning to live.

2

THE JOURNEY'S COURSE

Wʜᴇɴ ᴍʏ ᴍᴏᴛʜᴇʀ ᴅɪᴇᴅ, I was twenty-two, legally an adult but inwardly a child. I had refused to believe in death—by which I meant her death—even when she had become so frail that the long, graceful fingers that had taught me how to play a scale could barely graze my hand like the lightest summer leaf. I still refused, even when the nurse my father had hired to sleep beside her on the last, fitful nights of her life had showed me the stethoscope and said "I'm ready." Ready? Ready for what? I had wondered, not daring to ask, not wanting to know what final murmurs of the chest and heart, and then what final silence, she would hear. It was the nurse's job to be ready for that; I would never be ready.

In this way, the shock of mortality propelled me on a journey I wanted not to take, forced me to discover lessons I wanted to ignore. And then, suddenly, I could not ignore them any longer.

I think we each believe that the world begins with us, and that our loss is the first loss. We resist acknowledging that the history of loss is the history of life and that, as Shakespeare wrote, "all that lives must die, Passing through nature to eternity." It is a realization that may come with different force, depending on our age, circumstance, and personal family history, disrupting, heightening, challenging, or changing how we view ourselves and how we live our lives.

Even at the time, I dimly saw how the many ways in which I was changed and challenged by my mother's death both mirrored and heightened the natural crises of identity described by Erik Erikson in his theory of the life cycle. According to Erikson, there are eight "psychosocial" stages through which we may pass in the course of our life from birth to old age and death. Each stage is distinguished by its characteristic set of psychological and social concerns and by its own potential for crisis. In infancy, the conflict is between basic trust and mistrust; in early childhood, between autonomy and shame; at "play age," between initiative and guilt; at school age, between industry and inferiority; in adolescence, between identity and identity confusion; in young adulthood, between intimacy and isolation; in adulthood, between generativity and stagnation; and in old age, between integrity and despair.

At twenty-two, I straddled two stages—that of late adolescence, whose central theme is identity versus identity confusion, and that of early adulthood, whose major crisis focuses on intimacy versus isolation. These are also the phases of the life cycle in which the adult emerges from the child, asserting his autonomy and testing his independence from his parents even as he gropes for ways to remain connected to them. That balance between attachment and independence can be so difficult to achieve that for some the conflict can continue far into the next phase of the life cycle and beyond.

Further, because our identity is partly defined by the many roles we play throughout our lives, it is not surprising that the loss or threatened loss of any major role (in my case, the two roles as my mother's daughter and as Peter's girlfriend and perhaps wife) will shake, threaten, and unsettle even the most seemingly composed among us.

Thus, given the actual events of my own years of late adolescence and early adulthood, however out of sync I felt with my contemporaries, in some ways I was very much in sync with Erikson's abstract-sounding themes of conflict, crisis, and identity. To me, however, these conflicts were very real battles, faced every day: How could I be my mother's daughter, honoring her last wish to give up Peter, and still fulfill my commitment to Peter? Could I be child and adult, daughter and lover, all at once? Was there a single role that would bring all of these important yet conflicting identities together, or would they always remain a confused blur?

Having to confront—and feeling the urgency to resolve— so many crises of life, love, and loss all at once meant facing very real and immediate decisions about how I was to live my life and with whom, and who I was or would be: At Mom's death, I no longer could run to her arms to find the warm base of trust and security that her embrace had given me as a lasting legacy from infancy and early childhood. Would I ever find such security again? Perhaps, in Peter's arms . . . Yet that new foundation of intimacy and commitment had been threatened, too, as a result of Peter's still uncertain medical prognosis.

These questions of identity involved past, present, and future: Who was I in relation to my past—that is, to my mother? What sort of foundation would I be building for the future with Peter? Depleted and empty as I felt, what sort of foundation could I find within myself?

In this way, the traumas (or what psychologists call the "non-normative" events) of serious illness and death heightened, intensified, and telescoped the conflicts and crises of adolescence and early adulthood—stages that are generally said to extend until one's early thirties—into a two-year period that had ended by my early twenties. No wonder that I would sometimes listen to the casual concerns of my contemporaries as if through some long-distance wire, so that it seemed that they resided in a calmer place, which my life's different losses had forced me to tour too quickly or bypass altogether. For loss had propelled me into what seemed a separate phase of my own particular life cycle. "I made you grow up, Diane," Peter had joked tenderly shortly after his operation. But it was life itself that had made me both in sync and out of sync, a still blossoming adult and one of life's seasoned veterans all at once.

There was another way in which I was peculiarly in and out of sync. College and graduate school handily provide middle-class adolescents and young adults with what Erikson terms a psychosocial moratorium or respite from adulthood, a time in which to experiment with, rehearse, and refine the kind of person we wish to be when we actually begin our adult lives. As it happened, what would be for my peers at school a moratorium from the obligations of adulthood was for me a period filled with lessons and responsibilities of another order, so much so that even as I prepared at last to find my first job in the "real" world of work, it seemed that I would need a vacation, a break, perhaps an escape simply to assimilate all that had happened.

I did not realize yet that every mourner takes an enforced moratorium, whether he knows it or not. It is the period of mourning itself. Formally, the mourner may take off only a few days from work or school to attend the funeral and collect his thoughts, but inwardly a longer process begins, in which vital questions of meaning and identity become paramount.

"When the dead person has been, as it were, the keystone of a life," sociologist Peter Marris has written, "the whole structure of meaning in that life collapses when the keystone falls." However, even stripped of both meaning and structure, the mourner will gradually begin to seek in what was lost what Marris has called a "thread of continuity"—a lifeline that, as it unfurls over time, will help lead to the discovery of new meaning and purpose.

For me, all keystones had faltered at once: To what purpose would my love and care be directed now? To what family goals could I look, now that my family of origin had been shattered and the future of the man with whom I wished to build a new family remained a question? Now that I could no longer return to the home in which I had grown up, where would my home be? Now that I was no longer a student, where would I work? Who would *I* be now?

For every mourner the specific questions differ, but the crises remain similar. To love and to work are the fundamental goals of life, Freud wrote. But when death disrupts the cornerstones that hold our lives together, the foundation may not hold. That foundation is our identity, ourselves. That is why, Marris wrote, "The fundamental crisis of bereavement arises, not from the loss of others, but the loss of self."[1]

It is a crisis of identity, and a crisis of what one's life itself may mean. And if, as the Viennese psychoanalyst Viktor Frankl asserted, it is meaning itself that provides our very will to live, then it was no wonder that the terrible disarray I felt within found expression through so much sadness and despair. Frankl called this "will to meaning" man's primary motivation in life—a greater need than the pleasure principle or the sexual instinct. It is a search that may not be evident or conscious as we go about the ordinary business of daily life, but it is one that becomes paramount—as it did for me—when we are threatened by loss or face its aftermath.[2]

Ideally, out of the identity confusion so characteristic of adolescence comes an integrated sense of who we are and wish to be as an autonomous individual, as a partner in love, and as a part of a family of our own. Ideally, after the confusion and crisis of loss, new meaning will be found.

To my ears, such questions did not have the earnest, abstract sound of a late-night conversation in a college dorm. They had been dramatized and intensified by the very real shocks of life, by Mom's death and Peter's illness, and had shrouded me with vulnerability about a future in which I had once felt ignorantly secure.

[1] Peter Marris, *Loss and Change*, revised ed. (London: Routledge and Kegan Paul, 1986), 32–33.

[2] See Viktor E. Frankl, *Man's Search for Meaning*, 3rd ed. (New York: Simon & Schuster, 1984).

It was during this moratorium of mourning—a period filled with inner doubt and uncertainty—that I separated from Peter, and it was at its end that I decided that I must and would face any uncertainty with him. I have called it a moratorium, and in a certain sense I felt as if my life had been suspended at a particular moment of time, one in which everything that had once been familiar suddenly and cataclysmically had been transformed into something strange and unknown. But just as the infant toddler is propelled to explore the brave new world to which he has so recently been introduced, a mourner also must feel his way, restlessly searching within to discover what this new identity—as "mourner" or "bereaved daughter" or "widow"—actually means.

For me, that inner quest and conflict ultimately led to a new and different sense of who I was and would be. So much of the journey was lonely, taken in solitude even with Peter beside me. Yet I began to wonder who had gone before me and what they had found that was both like and unlike what I had found.

Quickly I realized that there have always been stories of loss. They begin in the Bible with Cain and Abel, and they touch on every conceivable kind of loss, through accident, illness, old age, or war, from Sarah's barrenness, to Jacob's grief for Rachel, to King David's mourning for his son Absalom.

I discovered countless modern works as well: Alfred Lord Tennyson poured out his sadness at losing his great friend A. H. Hallam in *In Memoriam*, and C. S. Lewis recorded his journey through grief after the death of his wife in *A Grief Observed*. All of Proust's *Remembrance of Things Past* can be seen as an attempt to recapture, in memory and on the printed page, an entire lost world. Then there are the many contemporary accounts of loss recounted in memoir and autobiography: *Death Be Not Proud*, John Gunther's haunting chronicle of his son's early death; Lynn Caine's story of her husband's death, *Widow*; Philip Roth's homage to his father, *Patrimony*; and, on a more philosophical note, *When Bad*

Things Happen to Good People, which grew out of Rabbi Harold Kushner's reflections on faith in the wake of his young son's fatal illness.

Not yet satisfied with my survey, I turned from classical and contemporary literature on loss to the psychological literature of loss. I found that many of the papers and research studies there tend to analyze data rather than dramatize it; they speak less to the heart than to the brain; and they often make for dry, overly abstract reading, even though a period of mourning so often draws upon the most urgent emotions of the heart.

Yet I also have found that it takes both human drama and the theory based on it to reveal fully both the masks of grief and the changed visage that can emerge afterward. The transformation is in some ways mystifying, as all change is. To chart and explain its course is a difficult task, but psychologists and other researchers have looked for patterns and found them. In the rest of this chapter I will explore this theory.

"By one of the dark ways behind the official consciousness my father's death has affected me profoundly. I had treasured him deeply and had understood him exactly. With his peculiar mixture of deep wisdom and fantastic lightness he had meant very much in my life. He had passed his time when he died, but inside me the occasion of his death has reawakened all my early feelings. Now I feel quite uprooted."[3]

Composed in response to a note of condolence, this letter may seem hardly remarkable. But the writer was Sigmund Freud; the year was 1896. Within a few months, Freud would begin both his self-analysis and his first major work, *The Interpretation of Dreams*.

Freud himself pointed out the connection between his fa-

[3] Quoted in Ernest Jones, *The Life and Work of Sigmund Freud, Vol. I, 1856–1900* (New York: Basic Books, 1953), 324.

ther's death and the new direction in his career in his 1908 preface to the second edition of *The Interpretation of Dreams*. The book, he wrote, "revealed itself to me as a piece of my self-analysis, as my reaction to my father's death; that is, to the most important event, the most poignant loss, in a man's life." For Freud, a new sense of what his life's work would be thus began to emerge after this most poignant loss. "His father's death was the stimulus," Freud's biographer Ernest Jones wrote. Having been "uprooted" emotionally by his father's death, Freud created new roots, of another kind, through his work.

Freud refrained from mentioning his personal response to this or any other loss in his 1917 paper "Mourning and Melancholia."[4] The emphasis instead is on how grief can go awry.

Freud considered grief a normal emotion and mourning a natural process, both best left to the mourner to live through without interference. In this vein he defined mourning as "the reaction to the loss of a loved person, or to the loss of some abstraction which has taken the place of one, such as fatherland, liberty, an ideal, and so on." Because grief is expected and in this sense ordinary, it follows, he wrote, that "although grief involves grave departures from the normal attitude to life, it never occurs to us to regard it as a morbid condition and hand the mourner over to medical treatment. We rest assured that after a lapse of time it will be overcome, and we look upon any interference with it as inadvisable or even harmful."

The process, however, is slow and painful. It unfolds over a protracted period of weeks or months suffused with feelings of dejection, loss of interest in the outside world, an inability to love, and the cessation of all but the most restless activity. Reality demands that the mourner "decathect" his "libido" from the "object." That is, he must acknowledge the reality of what has happened—that death has severed a treasured

[4] In *General Psychological Theory*, ed. Philip Rieff (New York: Collier Books. 1963).

attachment—and must now detach himself, letting go of the hands he once held with so much love. But because "man never willingly abandons a libido-position, not even when a substitute is already beckoning to him," the struggle will be difficult.

The reason is that reality is far too harsh to accept without protest. The facts of death conflict with our inner wish and fantasy—to deny that the loss has occurred. We wish life to go on as it has, and we wish to remain bound as before to a loved one with whom we have become intertwined. As a result, this detachment is accomplished only "bit by bit, under great expense of time and cathectic energy."

Bit by bit, the mourner reviews the past in memory. He calls forth, lingers over, and reflects on all the images, hopes, expectations, and regrets of that past. At first, they loom at the forefront of consciousness, and then, gradually, they recede until they become part of the past once more. In this way, what Freud called the "detachment of the libido" is accomplished.

In this way, also, the period of mourning passes and then fades. By contrast, melancholia—an emotional state that we would probably call depression today—morbidly lingers on.

Mourning and melancholia both begin with a loss, and both are painful to endure. But the Hamlet-like "melancholy that sits on high" can lead to despairing, obsessive, self-lacerating thoughts, eventually even to suicide. Because mourning and melancholia differ outwardly in these ways, Freud concluded, they also must differ in their origins.

Freud hypothesized that melancholia derives not so much from the death of a person as from a disappointment or loss of some unconscious object. The melancholiac may mourn the death of a person, but—more important, perhaps, to the unconscious—that person represents an idea, dream, wish, or fantasy that has been irrevocably lost.

Let us apply Freud's theory to a concrete example. A miscarriage or stillbirth is a very real loss. From the parents' perspective, it is far more than that; it is the death of a hoped-for future with that child. Similarly, infertility means more than the lost ability to conceive and bear children. It represents the death of a dream—the lost dream of a happy family life, biologically linking one generation to the next.

In recent years, clinicians have described the lingering self-blame and guilt often felt by couples who have experienced pregnancy loss or infertility. From a Freudian view, these mourners might be said to have internalized or come to identify with the lost object—their lost, never-to-be-born child or children—in a most complicated manner.

According to Freud, the process of identification in the wake of grief unfolds this way: First, the melancholiac identifies himself with the lost object—in this case, the lost child. Then he begins to criticize, not the lost person, but *himself*, with harsh, stinging, unremitting criticism that when looked at carefully, Freud believed, can be seen as actually directed not at the self but at the lost loved one. For infertile couples, the thinking may go like this: "I can't do anything right. I can't even bear a child!" Viewed from Freud's perspective, these thoughts might stand for an unspoken and still more anguished cry of pain, directed at the child in fantasy: "My child, why couldn't you *be* born!"

Thus, the despairing melancholiac appears to be criticizing himself while in reality he is lashing out at the person and, more than that, the idea or fantasy that he has lost. Using this unconscious disguise, the melancholiac can express his anger freely, Freud wrote. He is not criticizing the dead, after all. Far from attacking someone he loved and lost, he is blaming and criticizing himself.

Freud believed that this sort of identification between mourner and lost object takes place only in pathological mourning. Other analysts subsequently suggested that identification (though of a more benevolent sort) takes place in the normal course of mourning as well.

Still others pointed out more unusual aspects of grief. In 1937, Helene Deutsch described the seeming opposite of excessive grief in a paper titled "The Absence of Grief." Even when the sadness of grief is repressed or denied, Deutsch wrote, these feelings will find an outlet elsewhere—often in caring for others in their times of difficulty. Moreover, this "absence" of grief is actually a defense mechanism designed to shield a weak or threatened ego unable to acknowledge or cope with the reality of the loss.

English psychoanalyst Melanie Klein also elaborated on the relationship between loss and depression in her essay of 1940, "Mourning and Its Relation to Manic-Depressive States." Klein traced the origins of the sadness and pining of grief in older children and adults to the very young infant's anxiety over the loss of the mother's breast.

Thus, bit by bit, a still incomplete theoretical and clinical portrait of grief was being sketched. Then a terrible accident led the American analyst Erich Lindemann to address the subject in the mid-1940s.

———

On November 28, 1942, a grisly tragedy shook Boston. The Coconut Grove nightclub, filled to capacity, burned to the ground. Four hundred ninety-one people died; many others were hospitalized.

Tragic accidents often have the paradoxical effect of helping unknown others. Thirteen of the fire's grief-shocked survivors were treated by Erich Lindemann, then a psychiatrist at Boston's Massachusetts General Hospital. Listening, again and again, to the detailed accounts of charred horror would haunt anyone, but out of this experience came the thoughts and observations that made Lindemann's 1944 study "Symptomatology and Management of Acute Grief"[5] a landmark.

Lindemann is credited with being the first psychiatrist to identify a grief "syndrome"—a comprehensive range of emotions and symptoms that one could expect to encounter in the course of grief. Grief's outward symptoms, Lindemann wrote, include repeated sighing, exhaustion, and loss of appetite,

———

[5] *American Journal of Psychiatry* 101 (September 1944):141–48.

along with an inner sense of unreality, feelings of guilt, a preoccupation with thoughts of the deceased, and, finally, a confusing and ultimately exhausting state that fitfully alternates between physical restlessness and unfocused, listless apathy.

In many ways Lindemann's approach was like Freud's. Both observed that as intense as these feelings and symptoms appear at the time of loss, they will naturally and gradually subside. As the mourner reviews his relationship to the deceased, slowly he will free himself from the past and begin to move on. Usually, no psychiatric intervention will be necessary. When professional help is called for, a few brief sessions should do.

Like Freud, Lindemann took pains to contrast the course of "normal" grief with lingering responses that he considered to be morbid or pathological. He identified a long list of "distorted" reactions. These included the apparent absence of grief and delayed mourning described by Helene Deutsch; depression; expressions of angry hostility; a withdrawal from even sympathetic family members and from society in general; and a host of other self-destructive, self-defeating actions. Various medical symptoms might also turn up: symptoms similar to the deceased's last illness or psychosomatic conditions such as asthma or colitis.

Lindemann believed that eight to ten interviews over a course of four to six weeks with a trained psychiatrist should be enough to prevent many of the most severe responses. But the mourner's internal state should not be considered in isolation, he pointed out. What happens now if the person who died was the family's main breadwinner? What if you are a child, left suddenly without parents? The loss of an important figure in one's life, he noted more realistically than any of his predecessors, can be followed by "a profound alteration of the living and social conditions for the bereaved. In such cases readjustment presents a severe task quite apart from the reaction to the loss incurred."

Some psychologists have criticized Lindemann for charting

grief as a set, orderly, and time-limited process, one that the well-adjusted mourner will "get over" quickly, with hardly a look behind. But Lindemann's work also made more powerfully real than that of his predecessors the potentially devastating costs of grief gone awry, and it demonstrated the benefits of—and the potential importance of—preventive treatment.[6]

It did all this at the right historical moment—in 1944, in the middle of the most terrible war in human history. Loss and grief become an enduring legacy of any war, both for the soldiers returning home and for the countless friends and family members whose loved ones never return. Lindemann's reassurance that there is a normal and acceptable "grief syndrome" that will pass with time—or that a trained psychiatrist can help the mourner to overcome with time—must have been particularly welcome to practitioners serving a society eager to put the traumas of war behind, to return to normalcy, and simply to get on with life. Lindemann's model provided both understanding and hope. Soon, other researchers would build on Lindemann's groundbreaking work.

In late 1949, after spending five years as an army psychiatrist, a young child psychiatrist named John Bowlby returned to civilian life and was offered an opportunity that set the course for all his subsequent work: he was appointed a consultant to a research project, sponsored by the World Health Organization of the United Nations, on the special problems of homeless children. Bowlby was asked to study their mental health needs.

He published his findings in 1951, in the monograph *Maternal Care and Mental Health*, which stressed the potential ill effects on children of separation from their families, particu-

[6] "It is no exaggeration to say that [Lindemann's] work has colored all subsequent thinking about reaction to loss and has pointed the way to the prevention of mental illness by intervention services for people who have undergone a major loss": Colin Murray Parkes and Robert S. Weiss, *Recovery from Bereavement* (New York: Basic Books, 1983), 13.

larly from their mothers. "What is believed to be essential for mental health," Bowlby wrote in a work that was soon translated into a dozen languages, "is that the infant and young child should experience a warm, intimate and continuous relationship with his mother (or permanent mother-substitute) in which both find satisfaction and enjoyment."[7] The loss or absence of such care, he wrote, could prove devastating.

These principles, still in formation, were to become the cornerstone of Bowlby's influential theory of attachment behavior. Basically, the theory holds that strong, caring attachments early in life are necessary to yield a secure, self-confident adult. But if, by contrast, very early in life, we are separated from or permanently deprived of our first and most important attachment—to our mother, mother substitute, or other chief caregiver—then anxiety, anger, depression, or other serious and lingering psychiatric ills may follow. Even so, a well-suited, permanent loving substitute may help alleviate or avoid these ills, for a secure, enduring attachment from infancy or early childhood on is of the utmost importance.

As his theory formed in embryo, Bowlby took notice of other research. In America, at the Primate Laboratory of the University of Wisconsin, Harry and Margaret Harlow were developing some provocative conclusions about the devastating effects of maternal deprivation on rhesus monkeys. The Harlows found that when even well-fed monkeys were isolated at birth from their mothers and peers for prolonged periods of time, they might flourish physically, but they would be impaired in virtually every other way. When placed with other monkeys, they did not know how to play or otherwise interact with them. Similarly, if struck by a fellow monkey, they were unable to strike back. Because they knew nothing of mating behavior, they could not respond to another monkey's overtures and were unable to mate. Having lived in seclusion, they had had no opportunity to learn any of these things, nor did they appear to have more than a limited capac-

[7] John Bowlby, *Attachment and Loss*, Vol. I (New York: Basic Books, 1969), xi–xii.

ity to learn even when they were placed in the company of other monkeys at a later age.

The only attachment these monkeys seemed to form at all was to the gauze-covered pads at the bottom of their cages. The pads were soft to the touch and could be cuddled, much as a child hugs the teddy bear that provides a substitute for the warmth and closeness of his mother.

In a further experiment, the Harlows constructed two inanimate surrogate mothers, to be placed in the monkeys' isolation cages. One doll-like surrogate was wire mesh; the other was covered with terry cloth. The monkeys all rejected the wire-mesh dolls. Instead, they clung, cuddled, and became attached to the terry-cloth dolls. Physical comfort and security seemed as essential as social training and stimulation. These were all most effectively provided by the mother. Harry Harlow wrote Bowlby: "I am now quite convinced that there is no adequate substitute for monkey mothers early in the socialization process."[8]

For human infants, as for monkeys, attachment to the mother seemed paramount. For human infants, as for monkeys, separation from or loss of this primary attachment could be devastating. But how and why did such attachments develop? Were they ingrained, in some way instinctual? How else could such behavior—and these reactions to loss—be explained?

Work in another field altogether began to capture Bowlby's attention—the emerging discipline of animal behavior known as ethology. Bowlby took note in particular of the theories and research of Konrad Lorenz. Lorenz had observed the development (through the process known as imprinting) of strong attachments between very young ducklings and goslings and their mothers or substitute mother figures. Like the Harlows' monkeys, these animal species need and crave attachment.

[8] Bowlby, 165. For further discussion of the Harlows' experiments, see Roger Brown, *Social Psychology* (New York: The Free Press, 1965), 32–43.

Lorenz's work, Bowlby wrote, "revealed a new world, one in which scientists of high calibre were investigating in non-human species many of the problems with which we were grappling in the human, in particular the relatively enduring relationships that develop in many species, first between young and parents and later between mated pairs, and some of the ways in which these developments can go awry. Could this work, I asked myself, cast light on a problem central to psychoanalysis, that of 'instinct' in humans?"[9]

For Bowlby, the answer was yes. Moreover, his investigations in ethology led him to break with the classical Freudian point of view on an increasing number of issues, large and small, many of them having to do with the importance of attachment in human relationships.

According to Freud, it is the instinctual desire to satisfy the two primary drives for food and sex that chiefly powers human action. Attachments to others are important because they help fulfill these needs. Thus, relationships with others are of great significance, but viewed in this scheme they are secondary.

The work of Harlow and Lorenz and his own research now made Bowlby question Freud's model—to hypothesize that the need for attachment was primary, not secondary, and that the most crucial attachment of all is to the mother. Bowlby began to examine the course of attachment and the effects of loss on very young children. Before Bowlby, a number of theorists had assumed that children were not capable of feeling the depths of a loss as intensely as adults. Yet, Bowlby pointed out, many theorists also assumed that psychological difficulties in adulthood very frequently had their antecedents in troubling experiences—including separation and loss—in early life. How were early loss and later difficulties really connected? And how could these contradictory theoretical views be reconciled?

Rather than basing his theories, as others had, on analytic

[9] John Bowlby, *A Secure Base* (New York: Basic Books, 1988), 25.

sessions with adults remembering their childhoods from the distance of memory, Bowlby began by observing infants and young children themselves. He soon found that young children, when separated from their mothers even temporarily, respond first with loud, crying protestations. Eventually, the crying declines and fades, but in its stead despair and apathy set in. At this point, outwardly, the child will seem to have withdrawn from others. Inwardly, however, he will continue to yearn for the mother's presence. The signs of pining could range from a quiet, listless waiting for the mother's return to active "searching" for the lost mother—roaming from room to room—in solitary play. In such moments described by Bowlby, the mournful child is indeed the parent to the newly grief-stricken adult described by Lindemann.

Rationally, it would seem that nothing would make the despairing child happier than an actual reunion with the mother. In neither children nor adults, however, can emotions be counted on to be rational. Bowlby observed that when the mother did return—in some cases from a temporary absence owing to a hospital stay—often the child would become angry, remain withdrawn, or in some other way reproach and punish her for having left at all. If the mother did not return—if, most tragically, she had died—then even well-meaning, loving attempts by someone else to act in the mother's place would be greeted with similar shows. Anger, reproach, and rejection would reign until, finally, detachment, apathy, and dejection set in.

In Bowlby's observation, protest, despair, and detachment form the basic cycle of response to loss; frustration, anger, sadness, and despair can be the legacy of lost bonds. The damage can be repaired, but it requires both more time and more care than many theorists previously thought. Moreover, Bowlby believed, the course of mourning in children and adolescents closely resembles that in adults.

In any case, Bowlby did not see any evidence to support Freud's theory that identification with the lost person played a major role in mourning. Rather, the crying, protests, and seemingly pointless searching all represented a "persistent, though disguised, striving" to search out, call back, and recover the lost object.[10] Further, it was a pattern so deeply and universally ingrained that psychology alone could not account for it.

At this point, Bowlby turned from Freud, the founder of psychoanalysis, to Konrad Lorenz, the founder of modern ethology. Lorenz had hypothesized that animal species are genetically endowed with certain behavioral patterns needed for survival. And Bowlby saw a very precise survival pattern in the child's wail for his lost mother.

Like the very young of other mammals, human infants are helpless. Simply in order to survive, they require the basic care, protection, feeding, and shelter of other, older beings. If the young child were to lose his mother, he himself would quite literally be lost as well. Infants and toddlers notoriously follow their mothers everywhere. When the mother is even momentarily lost from sight, a child's cry urgently signals both his need and his distress. Such cries demand response; they are meant to. If none comes immediately, the child will crawl, walk, or run in search of Mother, until he either finds her or gives up in despair.

In this way, too, the mourner will yearn and cry and search for the loved one who was lost. This is the search on which every mourner embarks, and it was the search on which I embarked after my mother's death: first, the actual journey to Cleveland, to recover what memories and familial relationships I could; and then the longer, deeper journey within.

I hear myself in memory, weeping, and then I listen to my infant son erupt in tears as I take even one step to leave the room where he is playing. I think, The painful wail of the mourner is not so very different from the cries of children. It is only that, as adults, we recognize more fully than children the futility of hoping that our cries will bring the dead to life again or that an actual search will yield a similar recovery.

[10] Bowlby, *Attachment and Loss*, Vol. III, 30.

Still, we cry, pine, remember, and move restlessly about in our search to recover someone we have lost and cannot find—much as children do. Like children, too, we then vent rage, anger, sadness, and despair until, finally, the intensity of all these emotions diminishes. The realization sinks in that reality will not change, and so we must change instead, reordering both our lives and our attachments. Child or adult, this is the journey of grief.

———

After great pain, a new life emerges: That is this book's theme and refrain. But this theme derives not only from Emily Dickinson and from personal experience; it is grounded in the work of many theorists and clinicians. A variety of psychologists, psychiatrists, and sociologists have written about the journey through grief as a process of redefinition. In their work, they speak of changing identities, changing selves, and changing roles, each in the language of his or her particular discipline.

This is what they say:

Life in the wake of loss must become a new and different life—one, certainly, that acknowledges the past but one that also must yield, however painfully, to the changed reality of the present. Finally, there must be a recognition that because the present is different, both the future and our vision of it must be different, too.

We must learn to change, first, our daily living pattern—a pattern that now, suddenly, will not include someone or something that had previously been an important part of our lives.

Then, gradually, we must learn to change other, less tangible aspects of our lives and to find new resources, both practical and emotional, within—change certain roles, find a new identity, find a new self as we begin the journey of renewal and rebirth.

Phyllis R. Silverman, a leading researcher on widowhood who is currently codirector of the Child Bereavement Study at the Department of Psychiatry at Massachusetts General Hospital, has used the phrase "spoiled identities" to describe one of the chief consequences of loss.[11] Our relationships and attachments help us to define who we are; they help give us our identity. When we "lose" an attachment, we also lose a part of that identity. It is not uncommon, for instance, for mourners to speak of a loss as an amputation. The course of mourning, then, must also include the repair of that "spoiled" identity and, ultimately, the transformation into a new one.

But before finding our way to that new role, we must leave our old roles behind. Helen Rose Fuchs Ebaugh, professor and department chair of sociology at the University of Houston, has studied in detail the experience of "becoming an ex."[12] Although her study focused primarily on career changers (she herself is an ex-nun) and divorcés, many of her findings can be applied to the roles we must leave behind when death forces us to become widowed, parentless, or the mourner of other losses.

In the course of our lives, we each play many roles—as father, husband, son, executive, Little League coach. Losing any one role will leave a gap, and the more central the role is to our identity, the more confusion and crisis we will undergo. When the play whose script you have learned so well suddenly loses one of its leading characters, what role will you play now?

According to Ebaugh, at first it will be the role of the "ex-." It is one that may seem like an abyss, a void out of which no new role or purpose can ever come. But the role of the ex—the role of the mourner—is also one of transition, as you fully discover and master a new script with a new role.

Family, friends, and other relationships, including support groups, can prove extraordinarily helpful in assisting that

[11] Phyllis R. Silverman *Helping Women Cope with Grief* (Beverly Hills: Sage Publications, 1981). Although Silverman (who in part bases her views on the importance of attachment to identity on the work of feminist psychologists Jean Baker Miller and Carol Gilligan) applies her model primarily to women, I believe it holds equal validity for men.

[12] Helen Rose Fuchs Ebaugh, *Becoming an Ex: The Process of Role Exit* (University of Chicago Press, 1988).

transition. And when it is completed, you are no longer an "ex"; you are no longer a mourner. The past may always be with you, in some form of memory, but other roles and different aspects to your identity will now take precedence.

In their study of the newly widowed, British psychoanalyst Colin Murray Parkes and Robert S. Weiss, professor of sociology at the University of Massachusetts, found three distinct and conflicting identities available to the newly bereaved:

> First is an identity based on the assumption that the marriage continues. The widow or widower may refer to the spouse in the present tense as though the death had not occurred and may continue to consider the spouse's wishes and needs in household management or personal planning. Second is an identity based on the assumption that the spouse no longer exists and there is no further obligation to the spouse. Third is an identity based on the assumption that the spouse has been transported to another sphere but can still be affected, at least to some degree, by the bereaved individual's thoughts and behavior. This last identity is the one adopted by the "mourner."
>
> . . . Only as time passes and the work of relearning the world is carried out is the new widow or widower likely to lose this sense of fragmented identity and to feel relatively comfortable with one predominant identity."[13]

Although Parkes and Weiss studied only the widowed, the general process they chart can be applied to other losses as well.

What all these theories focus on, finally, is the loss of identity and the consequent loss of meaning. After all, a great part of the meaning in our lives involves relationships. When someone close to us dies, part of the practical purpose and everyday meaning to our lives is also lost. To "recover" from loss is in some sense to recover new meaning. To build a new identity is to create a new frame of meaning.

[13] *Recovery from Bereavement*, 160.

Further, the deep pain of mourning derives in large part from that very struggle to eke out some meaning from the loss.[14] It is also the struggle that leads us on the road to transformation.

We struggle to find that new role, often helped by the support of others, but it still remains a search for one's own identity as an individual. Then, finally, after pain and search, there may emerge not only a new self but one revitalized and refreshed. However, one may also return embittered, numb or wounded, in part or in whole. That is the struggle that we will find dramatized in the stories of others, and in our own.

[14] See Marris, *Loss and Change,* and Frankl, *Man's Search for Meaning.*

3

LOSS
AT AN EARLY AGE

"AFTER THE FIRST DEATH, THERE IS NO OTHER." These words conclude a well-known poem by Dylan Thomas, "A Refusal to Mourn the Death, by Fire, of a Child in London." It was written in 1945 and 1946, shortly after the close of a war that had caused so many deaths by fire. Each new death will bring forth public displays of mourning and lamentation, Thomas suggests. But for him, it is the very first death alone that will burn in memory—burn and burn again with the knowledge of each new death.

So it is for all of us, I think, whether we have lived through a world war or have waged more private battles. With each new loss we will relive, remember, or grieve once more at the thought of that very first loss. And the younger we are when that loss comes, the more heavily it weighs on everything that comes afterward.

———

On December 18, 1918, my father's father took the local streetcar from the small Virginia town of Portsmouth into Norfolk. He never saw his home again.

That evening, he had gone to hear a speech by the fiery populist orator William Jennings Bryan. An immigrant general store owner from Lithuania and the principal of the Hebrew school in his small Southern community, my grandfather always enjoyed such talks.

Afterward, he boarded the streetcar to go home. He had traveled the route a thousand times since he had settled his family in the small house just off High Street and Second Avenue. And as usual, when the streetcar bell rang and the car jolted to a halt, he had climbed off the last steep step and turned to walk the final block home.

Suddenly, a man with a gun ran up to him. It was never certain whether my grandfather knew the man or not. It was dark, and it all happened so quickly. My grandfather was thirty-six years old.

It was eleven o'clock when the two gunshots rang out. They woke my father, sleeping at home, less than a block away.

The sound awakened other neighbors as well. And it was the neighbors who found the body lying in the street, recognized it, and, accompanied by the police, carried it back to my father's house—now the dead man's house.

They placed the body, face up, on the dining room table. Seventy years later, my father cannot talk about that sight without covering his eyes—covering them, so he will not see that sight again: the dead man's glassy, wide-eyed stare that blindly gazes on his wife, his three sons, and his two-year-old daughter.

Now my father uncovers his eyes only to turn and look away, perhaps to look back once again, still transfixed in memory by the oddly unfamiliar set to his father's once familiar face. Yes, it was his father, but it was no longer his father. His father was dead, and nobody—no doctor, no rabbi, no wife, no son or daughter—could ever mend the wound, or sew back the soul in this lifeless thing.

Children believe in magic in a way that no adult can, but what had caused this, the cruelest magic imaginable? What crime had he committed, my father wondered, that could demand so dreadful a punishment, meted out, like lightning, by God himself?

To my father, it always seemed as if the two gunshots had also killed and arrested a part of his life. Nine-year-olds—especially nine-year-olds who, like my father, are the oldest of four children—are often admonished to act like young men. And now he was the "man of the family."

But he was only a child. Just a few minutes before, he had been asleep, dreaming of childish things. Just the previous night, he had laughed at Charlie Chaplin and held his father's hand as they walked home from the theater in town. Now this last frame in memory, like the silent frames to the movie, would be frozen in time, forever. There would be no new scenes to live and play through with his father, no more movies, no more *Shoulder Arms*—not even an older man's shoulder on which to cry or lean for momentary support. And these dual burdens—of a stunted childhood and an unwanted early manhood—would weigh on him throughout his childhood, his adolescence, and, in some not always well hidden part of him, throughout the rest of his life.

"It changed my life forever," Dad tells me now, looking back on his younger self from the age of seventy-nine.

How could it not? Growing up, I heard the story—a terrible family fairy tale—only in bits and pieces. I am still piecing it together now, even as Dad himself tries to piece it together in memory, in conversation, and in the pages of the autobiography he has begun to record in recent years. What is clear is that an entire world shattered for him on that winter night in 1918, and not he, or his mother, or all the members of his family could ever put it back together again.

Yet these are the pieces that emerge from memory:

In the numb days that followed that first night of horror, perhaps it was fortunate that Jewish law provided so much structure to his life and to the whole family's life. Ritual required that the body be buried as soon as possible, and so the funeral took place the next day. Then, when the family came home from the cemetery, they sat on low chairs for seven days—the custom of sitting *shivah*. During that time, also according to custom, friends and neighbors and relatives would visit and extend condolences. They would tell stories of the deceased, to help the mourners remember, and then talk of other things, to help them forget. They would cook and feed and tend them at a time when they had no strength or will to do anything, anything at all. In that house, as in every house of mourning, the mourners in their low chairs would be set apart. But the community would also be there. And for those first seven days, the mourners who had been left so alone by their father and husband would not be alone, not be abandoned.

But seven days pass quickly, even when they are leaden with grief. Then life must begin again—an eerie new life in which the setting, the season, and all the outward details may at first seem unchanged, except that the center is missing, and with it, all joy or cheer.

For my father, each day now began and ended with another reminder of just how different life without his father would be. He would rise at six o'clock each morning to attend morning prayers before school and recite the mourner's *Kaddish*, as required by Jewish law and custom. Then, after school, he would return to the small *shul* once more to say *Kaddish* at the evening service. This was his duty and his responsibility as the "man" in the family—at least, as the oldest male. But it also meant that he had no time to play, to be the little boy he desperately wished to remain.

Life went on in Portsmouth, but without his father to guide him, my father felt lost, and the whole family was lost. For my grandmother Rose, it was as if, having crossed one sea to settle in America, she now found herself stranded in another country entirely—the country of widowhood. Once there, she found, there was no insurance, only four young children to support. There was some property, however—the general store and two houses next door which her husband had rented out. And propelled by her children's needs and her own steely determination, she "got on with life" with so much speed and energy that she would never have time to look back again. She reopened the store, rented her property, and before long married the young man whom she had hired (the relative of another relative from Baltimore) to help her run the store.

In this way, my grandmother tried, Dad tried, the whole family tried to find themselves again. They found that they would never have their old life back, but they constructed a new and different life, and even welcomed a new father, whom they affectionately called "Pop."

Still, throughout this time and for years later, Dad suffered what he now calls "identity problems." Within a year of his own father's death, a classmate and friend lost his father to the influenza epidemic. But the friend's remaining family could not care for him, and he was sent away to live in an orphanage. Dad visited and wondered: Could this still happen to him?

At the same time, an older neighbor, the mother of another schoolmate, watched my father grieve and began inviting him to join her family for their Seventh-Day Adventist church meetings. The meetings—perhaps it was just the idea of belonging, even momentarily, to a family that was whole and intact—brought him comfort. And, vulnerable and in need of solace, for a time Dad was tempted to convert.

Still, from the day his father was murdered, Dad had vowed he would become a doctor. Not only would *he* have a new life, so would the many children he would deliver into the world, once he became an obstetrician. So would the many other patients he would heal and bring back to life, even as he had not been able to heal his father.

At the same time, he would move out of this town and out of this state—a terrible place where little boys could lose their fathers in an instant, and where he might unwittingly treat and save the life of the man who had killed his father. He would get away from the past, put it out of his sight forever. He would move to Baltimore and start his practice there.

He would even change his name, from Abraham Coin (a Southern spelling for Cohen) to a name that did not invite the anti-Semitic taunts that had plagued him growing up. And so, after receiving his medical degree and moving to Baltimore, he became Alfred Joseph Cole, M.D. He had chosen "Cole," Dad explained to me years later, because it is the first word of the traditional Hebrew song *"Hatikvah,"* "The Hope."

He became Alfred Joseph Cole, M.D., a new man, a grown man now and one with a medical purpose to fulfill that would also satisfy the deepest magical wish—the wish to save life—of the little boy who had watched helplessly when the body of his father was carried into his house so many years before.

But the child is father to the man, Wordsworth said, and the man who continues to practice medicine at the age of seventy-nine is also the boy who had vowed to escape the scene of his father's death. As I listen to Dad's story, I now see the man who was driven to show his love for his own three children through the financial security he could provide for us, often working seven days a week—and sometimes, it seemed, seven nights a week as well. Growing up, I resented those hours desperately, but he worked this hard, I see now, to escape his personal demons, to demonstrate unequivocally that he would never abandon his children—certainly not financially—the way his father, however unwillingly, had abandoned him.

I listen some more, and now I see the little boy peek through in the man who has always promised his own three children that he would live forever: "I'm going to live to be a hundred and twenty," he likes to say. It is a way of also saying that he will never orphan us, will never allow us to be fatherless.

And it is this same lost little boy whose immediate response to any setback, whether trivial or traumatic, will be to ask, repeatedly, bewilderingly, in the injured tone of the victim, "Why does everything have to happen to *me?*" Because starting at the age of nine, I now see, it must have seemed to him that everything most certainly had happened to him, and what's more, it kept on happening, a nightmare that never went away.

"It changed my life forever," Dad repeats. "If Dad hadn't

died," he says wistfully. "If Dad hadn't died . . . " And as I listen, I can only be grateful that my father is still here to tell me his tale, in love and in pain.

———

Everyone's story is different, but listening to Dad, I can't help thinking of another Southern tale, James Agee's Pulitzer Prize–winning autobiographical novel, *A Death in the Family*. In that true-life story, six-year-old Rufus (a stand-in for Agee) must grapple with his father's sudden death. Rufus's father is not murdered but dies suddenly in a freak auto accident; the city is Knoxville rather than Portsmouth; and the year is 1915 instead of 1918. The details differ, but the emotional atmosphere, as well as the psychological toll and turmoil, has always struck me as being nearly identical to what occurred in my father's life. Even the little details of that era's small-town Southern milieu, like the Charlie Chaplin movie that opens the novel, strike familiar chords.

James Agee and my father were both born in 1909. Both saw their early tragic loss as the formative experience of their lives—the one event that shaped them and that they could never escape. Both felt "lost" in the wake of their loss, and in its aftermath, throughout their lives, both sought some kind of transforming refuge in their work—my father as a physician, Agee as a poet, novelist, and journalist. Dad had his "identity problems," and, to judge by the reckless life recounted in Laurence Bergreen's biography, so did Agee, who went from being a troubled if gifted adolescent to a more troubled, more brilliant adult.[1] Yet for all his talent, Agee himself never seemed convinced that anything he did was good enough. Or perhaps he simply could never allow himself to let go of a cherished work—abandon it as he, his father's cherished offspring, had been abandoned. And so Agee was always revising, revising, and revising yet again both his novel (left unfinished at his death) and his impassioned jour-

———

[1] Laurence Bergreen, *James Agee: A Life* (New York: E. P. Dutton, 1984).

nalistic portrait of Southern farmers trapped by the Depression, *Let Us Now Praise Famous Men*, a work that at one point, Bergreen recounts, Agee had gone so far as to drive into New York to show to his publisher—before turning the car around and taking his manuscript back to his desk to work on some more.

Agee seemed to find it difficult to finish any piece of work he deeply cared about, yet at the same time he seemed hellbent on finishing his life prematurely: He was a self-destructive alcoholic, who chain-smoked, contemplated ways to commit suicide, and never seemed to be happy in a marriage or an affair until he had succeeded in making it go sour.

Dad's loss was always with him, as was Agee's, yet Dad never veered toward self-destruction or was drawn by death's lure, as Agee seemed to be. In fact, Dad turned so far the other way that his carefully balanced diet, aversion to cigarette smoke, and fastidious teetotaling have long since passed into family lore. Some of my most vivid—and embarrassing —childhood memories are of Dad vehemently lecturing friends, and sometimes even passing strangers, that they were endangering their most precious possession, their health, every time they smoked, drank, or ate red meat—the voice of good medical sense today, but at that time (the 1950s and 1960s) the dire warning of a crank.

As I listen to Dad and then think about Agee, I can't help but wonder not only at their similarities but at their differences. Or was it the same fascination with death that drew Agee to his reckless consumption of tobacco and alcohol, and terrified Dad? How does it happen that two people, faced with similar catastrophes at approximately the same time in their lives, respond in such diverse ways?

Such similar yet different stories point up the difficulties that not just I, as a daughter and writer, but social scientists, too, have encountered in trying to assess the ramifications of loss at an early age. Common sense tells us that early loss must be tremendously important. At the very least, it will always be a fact that cannot be erased.

But a grief that persists longer than the time it takes to

"climb back in the saddle" is often looked upon by society in general, and even by professionals, as bordering on the unhealthy, if not the pathological. "Put the past behind you," friends and family counsel; it does not matter how young or old you are, how recently or long ago the loss occurred.

What gets lost in this wishful formula, however, is the fact that grief, like physical injury, will leave scars that can cause pain, months, years, and sometimes decades later. Yet several years ago, when I called to interview a chaplain who specialized in grief counseling for an article I was then researching on parental loss, our initial conversation went something like this:

Grief Counselor: You know, I just don't understand why you're writing this article. Are your parents alive?

Diane: Well, my mother died several years ago.

Grief Counselor: Ah, I thought so! Several years ago! And still not over it!

No, and I suppose I never did and never will get over it, if "getting over it" means forgetting my mother's legacy to me both in life and in death.

Trained though he was, this grief counselor, like so many untrained sympathetic well-wishers, seemed to have accepted several common misconceptions about grief: that grief is something that you do "get over"; that a healthy person surely will get over it in a relatively brief, prescribed period of time; and that once you have done so, your mind and heart will be free of ghosts forever.

In my research, however, I found that far more common than stories of people "getting over" grief were accounts such as these: "These past three and a half years since his loss have been the most difficult period in my life," former Congresswoman Bella Abzug recently wrote in a memoir of her husband, Martin. "I still have this tremendous pain. . . . I haven't found any five stages, just tremendous sadness."[2]

---

[2] Bella Abzug, "Martin, What Should I Do Now?" *Ms.*, July/August 1990, 95–96.

A woman whose adult son committed suicide seven years ago said: "His life left wreckage. . . . I'm fine in many ways, but then there's still this wreckage. . . . "

And at lunch one day, a professional acquaintance suddenly burst into tears as she began recounting the story of the still-birth of her son, fourteen years before. "I don't think about this often anymore," she apologized, "but when I do, it still hurts so much."

Nor am I alone in hearing this refrain. Patricia Weenolsen, a professor of psychology at the University of California at Santa Cruz, whose special area of interest includes the impact of loss over the course of the life span, has written: "We can never completely 'get over' a major loss in the sense that all its effects are negated, that it is 'forgotten.' Our losses become part of who we are, as precious to us as other aspects of our selves, and so does the transcendence of those losses."[3]

Similarly, Don Scharf, a psychotherapist based on Long Island who specializes in issues of loss, adoption, and infertility, has found in his practice that the period of mourning is much longer than one year. In some cases, he asserts, it may even take generations to absorb a family's legacy of loss: "There are losses that transcend generations. . . . In fact, look at you," Scharf told me. "The true birth of your book was in 1918, Diane, on the night your grandfather disappeared."

Every loss is a fact that cannot be altered. Dad's loss was a fact of his life, and as I grew up, it became a fact of mine. My mother's mother had lost her mother to influenza when she was eight or nine, and both stories together left me with a terror of the obscure, unknown forces that could tear a parent out of your life forever. For me, these family losses at one remove intensified a common childhood fear of the monsters and witches of fairy tales. What must my father and my

[3] Patricia Weenolsen, *Transcendence of Loss Over the Life Span* (New York: Hemisphere Publishing, 1988), 57.

grandmother have felt when the lightning bolt hit them directly? The shock of its force resonated through their lives and later through mine, not only as a child who must be ever vigilant against invisible witches capable of stealing a loved parent from me, but as an adult whose struggles to make sense of losses of my own gave new force to buried family memories from long ago.

A number of researchers, psychiatrists, and psychotherapists further confirm what family history suggests: that an early loss is not so easily forgotten or erased in the rush of all that comes after. Rather, it is absorbed, with some wounds healing more quickly and wholly than others, and some scars remaining or becoming more stubbornly visible at certain times in life than at others.

This is one of the underlying themes of a study by Phyllis Silverman on the impact of a parent's early death on women of college age.[4] Silverman conducted in-depth interviews with eighteen college upperclasswomen, graduate students, and students returning to college at an older age. The women fell into three groups, based on the age at which the loss occurred:

There were those women who were grade school age or younger when the death occurred. Although most of them were not in any sense in mourning, the death was still a factor in their lives. They were trying to find a place in their adult identity for their deceased parents. A second group were those who lost their parent during the teenage years. They seemed to be dealing still with remnants of a grief reaction that was causing them some stress. They described feelings of anger and sadness. The third group of five women, whose parent died while these women were at college, were still experiencing aspects of acute grief. They were tearful and had difficulty talking.

[4] Phyllis R. Silverman, "The Impact of Parental Death on College-Age Women," *Psychiatric Clinics of North America* Vol. 10, No. 3 (September 1987): 387–404.

Regardless of how long ago the loss occurred, and regardless of the daughter's age at the time, the loss continued to be felt, and felt again, in each of these women's lives. In this sense, none of them had "got over it."

Rather, Silverman found, as life went on and the circumstances and concerns of each woman changed, different questions and issues arose that could not have been addressed earlier but must be addressed now, for the first time. The questions have to do with identity and the very meaning of who "I" will be or can be now: How will I be a mother, without my own mother to help teach me how? Is it all right to be a career woman, when my mother gave up her own career to have me? What would she say, were she here? Unable to settle these issues in life, the young women often imagined continuing inner conversations with their dead, even as I did and continue to do in moments of special sadness or joy to this day. Thus, Silverman concluded, the impact of early parental loss "seems to last over the child's lifetime, affecting how other life cycle events are experienced and coped with."

Instead of viewing this reawakening—and new resolution —of a sense of loss at different stages in life as neurotic or pathological, Silverman has placed it in a different perspective: as part of the continuing process of bereavement—a process that leads not to recovery but to change:

> I have proposed elsewhere that adults do not recover from their grief but are changed by it. In the accommodation they make to this loss, they must deal with those changes. . . . The same process holds for children as well. Some of their accommodation may have to wait until they have matured sufficiently to deal with the many issues raised by the death. Some, even ten years later, are still working on accepting the death and its finality. . . .
> One way of explaining . . . is to call it unfinished business. . . . I would suggest, instead, that [these reactions are] part of the work they needed to do as young adults. They needed to understand how their parent's death affected them as they developed their identity as adults.

Indeed, the lessons I learned in the year of Peter's illness and Mom's death would continue to provide guidance for each of the losses that came later, and will continue to do so, in good times as well as in bad, as long as my life continues.

In addition, regardless of the individual's age when the loss occurred and regardless of how long ago it was, Silverman found several other common themes. One was a feeling of being isolated from and out of step with classmates and contemporaries—feelings my father experienced after his father's death, and feelings very similar to mine as someone who was "out of sync" with my contemporaries in college, graduate school, and after. This sense of solitude can also set the stage for responses to setbacks or losses later in life.

Loss at an early age, Bowlby wrote, "can sensitize an individual and make him more vulnerable to setbacks experienced later, especially to loss or threat of loss." Not everyone will become more vulnerable, Bowlby emphasized. However, three variables in a child's response to early grief are especially important in influencing and predicting the course of later mourning:

> (a) the causes and circumstances of the loss, with especial reference to where and what a child is told and what opportunities are later given him to enquire about what has happened;
> (b) the family relationships after the loss, with special reference to whether he remains with the surviving parent and, if so, how the patterns of relationship are changed as a result of the loss;
> (c) the patterns of relationship within the family prior to the loss, with special reference to the patterns obtaining between the parents themselves and between each of them and the bereaved child.[5]

Seeking to find a more tangible cause and effect between early loss and adaptation to life in adulthood, British sociolo-

[5] John Bowlby, *Attachment and Loss, Vol. III, Loss: Sadness and Depression* (New York: Basic Books, 1980), 310-11.

gist George W. Brown examined the possibility of a traceable link between the early loss of a parent and various psychiatric disorders in later life.[6] In two separate studies, Brown and his colleagues interviewed depressed women along with a large control group of nondepressed women in different London neighborhoods. Comparing the groups, he found in both studies that the loss of a mother by death or separation before the age of seventeen, and especially before the age of eleven, could indeed increase the woman's vulnerability to clinical depression in later life. However, the history of early loss would increase the risk of depression in adulthood only when what Brown termed a "provoking agent"—an "important loss or disappointment"—was also present in adulthood.

One of the most common provoking agents, though not the only one, he found, was premarital pregnancy. But why should the mere fact of pregnancy, without loss, have this effect? The reason, he suggested, may have to do with "the fantasy that becoming pregnant will somehow compensate for the closeness of the mother-child relationship of which the woman herself was deprived."

In her study of college women, Silverman, too, found that there was a tendency to relive earlier losses at critical times later in life. In my case, as well, I found myself grieving after each pregnancy loss not only for a lost child but for my mother all over again, for in losing the chance to become a mother I was also losing the chance to understand, remember, and become close to my mother in a new and different way. And in fact, now that I am a mother, I have reclaimed that part of my mother within me. In these ways, the first death stays with us in memory, resounds in new keys, and also can be resolved with different harmonies throughout our lives.

----

[6] George W. Brown, "Early Loss and Depression," *The Place of Attachment in Human Behavior*, ed. Colin Murray Parkes and Joan Stevenson-Hinde (New York: Basic Books, 1982), 232–68.

What seems to matter most in coping, both at the time of the parent's death and later, is the care, support, and understanding that the child receives from the surviving parent, family members, and other caregivers. I cannot think of a more poignant dramatization than Sarah Moskovitz's chronicle of the adult lives of child survivors of the Holocaust, *Love Despite Hate.*[7]

For the Jewish children of school age and younger who survived the Nazi Holocaust, there were frequently no parents, family members, friends, or any community at all to whom to turn after rescue from the death camps or emergence from the secret hiding places where some of these children had found shelter during World War II. Having no home of their own, twenty-four of these children came under the care of Alice Goldberger, a German refugee in England who, with the sponsorship of Anna Freud, established a secure and innovative group home for them in the peaceful village of Lingfield. The children ranged in age from three to eleven. Some were adopted; a few were found by and reunited with surviving family members. The rest continued to call Lingfield their home.

Thirty years later, Moskovitz, a therapist and college professor in California, sought out and interviewed these children as adults. Her group portrait is a testament not only to the importance of the continuing commitment of Alice Goldberger to the children's well-being but also to the resilience and adaptability of the human spirit. Despite their devastating early childhoods, Moskovitz found that most of the survivors had managed to create relatively satisfying adult lives. Some were lonely or had difficulty in forging new relationships, and some carried the burden of their past more heavily than others. But at the time of her interviews, only one was confined to a psychiatric hospital; another had become involved with drugs, and one had turned to crime.

Did the majority, then, "get over" their terrible childhood

[7] Sarah Moskovitz, *Love Despite Hate* (New York: Schocken Books, 1983).

losses? "The loss of parents in early life means loss of the very nucleus of one's own identity," Moskovitz wrote. For these children, many other markers of community identity and belonging were lost as well. As a result, it should be no wonder that the search to regain or reinvent an identity, to find a place or a family where they truly belong, has resonated throughout the subsequent lives of each of these child survivors. Indeed, Moskovitz asked, how could this personal history not continue to play some part in each one's life?

In fact, for most of these survivors, building a secure family home and having children of their own took on an almost mystical significance. Having lost or been deprived of a secure sense of place and self as children, they would find it as adults within a stable home and family life. For some, the goal was quite conscious; for others, these needs were acted out unawares. Naming a new child in memory of a dead parent—and in that way bringing the dead to life again—became a symbolic act of great significance. Many of these survivors discovered links to their family's past through a connection to Israel and in religious belief. Most of all, continuing to live and be fruitful in spite of all the horrors that they and their families had suffered became more than just an act of revenge against those who would annihilate them. It was a personal affirmation of life and a quiet claim of victory for the entire extended family that they mourned. In all these ways, they found new families to be part of, new homes and communities to call their own, and new identities for themselves.

Moskovitz's interviews underscored her belief that, Bowlby notwithstanding, the psychoanalytic literature has placed too much emphasis on the early mother-child relationship as the be-all and end-all of early development, while not placing enough importance on the role of supportive others. It is certainly true that the child survivors whom she interviewed as adults had benefited greatly from the nurturing presence of such an "outsider" in the form of Alice Goldberger, as well as from the support of the large extended family that the group home provided.

Perhaps just as important, these true survivors, Moskovitz

found, all possessed "a quality of stubborn durability. . . . They keep hoping, they keep trying to make the best of their lives. . . . Their hardiness of spirit and their quiet dignity are part of this persistent endurance. And enduring is, after all, most fundamental."

Moskovitz's provocative investigation sheds much light, but it does not answer still elusive questions: Why do some children develop that "stubborn durability," that "hardiness of spirit," while others do not? Why do some children fare better through the years than others?

One of the larger, long-term studies to examine why some adults may feel the effects of early loss more acutely than others was recently led by psychiatrist Alan Breier, assisted by researchers at the National Institute of Mental Health.[8] Breier's research team interviewed ninety men and women who had suffered the loss of one or both parents between the ages of two and seventeen, along with a control group of twenty-three people who had not. As in Brown's study, early loss seemed to make people more vulnerable to serious depression later in life. But that vulnerability seemed to have little to do with the sex of the child, the sex of the parent, or the age of the child when the parent died. Instead, what mattered most was the kind of care and support the child received from other family members in the wake of loss.

The more emotional support and understanding the child received at the time, the less likely he or she was to fall prey to depression later in life. However, the more responsible the child felt for providing emotional support to the surviving parent, the more at risk the child was for depression in adulthood.

These findings point toward ways to heal the wound and minimize the pain of continuous hurt. But what does "emotional support" and help for the child actually mean?

Imagine the scene: The surviving parent, grandparents,

[8] Alan Breier, John R. Kelsoe, et al. "Early Parental Loss and Development of Adult Psychopathology," *Archives of General Psychiatry* 45 (November 1988): 987–93.

and other adults are no doubt feeling their own pain, fear, and shock in the wake of the death of someone they love. They may be feeling just as helpless as their children, and yet they must guide their children. They do not know what words of comfort or explanation to offer to themselves, much less to others. How do they tell a child? What do they say? And when? Deciding to "protect" the child (and perhaps also themselves), they may decide to say nothing. Or they may further rationalize their silence, saying the children aren't old enough to understand, anyway.

But many psychiatrists point out that though children may not yet possess the mental or intellectual capacity to "understand" the finality of death the way adults do, they feel the pain caused by a parent's absence no less harshly. In fact, the pain may ache even more, precisely because they cannot grasp what happened to the parent on whose caregiving presence they have learned to depend. For a child surrounded by so much wordless grief and fearful magic, it's no wonder that it may take years even to begin to repair the hurt and heal the wounds of early loss. Thus, concluded the Australian psychiatrist Beverley Raphael, for the young child who loses a parent, "The painful crisis of the death is just the beginning of a long period of readjustment."[9]

Even in this atmosphere, however, there are possibilities for solace and repair. "What seems to be important is the way the surviving parent continues to parent," Phyllis Silverman noted in her study on the impact of parental loss on college women. "Appropriate parenting, in part, means that the children feel cared for and are not put in the inappropriate position of having to care for their parent instead. The children need to feel they are respected so that as they grow they have enough sense of self to cope with each new stage and phase of the life cycle as well as with the changing impact of their parent's death."

[9] Beverley Raphael, "The Young Child and the Death of a Parent," Parkes and Stevenson-Hinde, 131–49.

In part, that respect can mean allowing bereaved children to express their emotions in their own way—emotions that may include anger, withdrawal, even a denial that the death has occurred. Almost all professionals now stress the importance of being honest, of finding some way to include the child in the funeral, and at the very least of answering questions and explaining what happened in terms that the child can understand. The point is that the child's tears and sadness should not be deemed a shameful secret. Death should not be seen as an evil punishment for which the child may blame himself. And death should not be shrouded in so much silence that a precious part of the child's heritage and identity—who his mother or father was and how the dead parent had lived —will seem to have died as well.

Several individuals talked to me about the lasting effects of silence and early loss.

"It was devastating—an irreparable loss," Mary[10] says. Her tone is a mixture of the vulnerable and the matter-of-fact. She pauses to look around her comfortably furnished apartment, its white walls covered with bookshelves, family photographs, brightly colored art posters. "When you lose a parent so young, you spend the rest of your childhood grieving for what you don't have, and you spend your early adulthood with the repercussions. And the thing that's so hard is that when your parent dies when you're so young, your memory is frozen in time, limited to the memories of a little child. And as you get older, those memories also fade."

When her mother died, Mary was only nine, but one image of "Mommy," as Mary calls her—she never had the chance to change to "Mom" or "Mother"—is frozen in the photograph she now hands me. In it, a slim, dark-haired woman in a white blouse and black skirt hovers over a chubby, grinning two-

[10] Mary's name and profession have been changed to ensure confidentiality. Where noted with an asterisk, details have been changed for other people interviewed for the book.

year-old whose wide eyes seem oblivious of everything but her attentive mother. "In my memory of her, she is this grandly grown-up person," Mary tells me with a nervous laugh and an expansive wave of the hand. "And she's only my age, the age I am now."

Yet at thirty-one, Mary's present age, her mother was on the verge of becoming ill. I glance from the photograph to look at Mary and see the resemblance: Mary is a perky, dark-haired, dark-eyed woman wearing faded blue jeans and a brightly colored T-shirt. Her words come in quick, staccato spurts, and as she kicks off her sandals and leans back in her wicker chair, you'd say she's twenty-five at most, a wide-eyed street-smart kid fresh out of college, not a lawyer who is well on her way to becoming a partner at a prestigious big-city firm.

My impression of her as we spoke one late-summer afternoon was of an energetic, insistently buoyant woman as eager for love as for success. Clearly, Mary has worked hard to be the tough adult, with her spunky, unflappable tone, and so there is a sense of poignant incongruence as she speaks of "Mommy," a figure frozen in time, frozen in memory. "She was my mommy, who took care of me, picked me up from school, took me to the park, took me for ice cream, taught me how to ride a bike and roller-skate."

And then Mommy died.

With an odd composure born of familiarity, Mary describes the grisly symptoms of her mother's final illness—a rare disease of the nervous system that left her so frail and brittle that by the end of her swift decline, she looked as if she were closer to sixty than to forty. The details spill out: Facts are something tangible to hold on to, Mary explains, and she has amassed them, fact by fact, as an adult, by going through medical texts and other books on her own.

She has had to embark on this part of her "search" as an adult—quite literally to search out the facts of her mother's death—because, she tells me, when she was a child the atmosphere was "very hush-hush. We didn't know Mommy was going to die until the week before, and even then we were not allowed to discuss it with her! And if there is anything I would tell people, it is to not make it all a secret!

"Afterward, I had a very hard time crying," she continues. "I knew that she had gone away, but I had a fantasy that she would come back. That she had been in Africa or something —on a trip—or in a plane crash. . . .

"No, things weren't shared with us for a long time. It was all hushed up. If I could have had *any* kind of discussion with her . . ." She pauses, in a silence filled with anger and wistfulness. "If I could have had *any* kind of discussion with her, that could only have helped."

Instead, as in a Victorian novel, the atmosphere remained "hush-hush," with Mary's father insisting on the "stiff-upper-lip" attitude that life must go on. He was "a man who was not comfortable talking about his feelings," Mary repeats throughout our conversation. Couldn't she ask him questions? I inquire. She shakes her head, shrugs. "It's very hard to get real mad at him when your father is all you have," she says simply.

In addition, there was a feeling that "you have to do well in school, and you have to have a lot of friends, and you have to keep very busy, and everything has to be terrific. And I was very angry, but I had to keep myself together and be a good little girl."

And so, outwardly, she made sure to play the "good little girl" who never asked, only performed. But inwardly, she asked, "Why me?" and questioned why she must live a childhood out of sync with her friends and classmates. "I had the feeling that I was the only one," Mary says. "There was a real sense of stigma, a sense that I had changed, that I had deepened and had feelings that others could not understand."

Certainly, she felt, no friends could understand her loss. Around them—each with a mother and a father to be present for them—she felt isolated, felt that she had to keep her emotions "bottled up." And even (or perhaps especially) the adults who could or should have understood would not allow her to play any role but that of a brave little girl. That included not only her father but also, Mary says sadly, her grandmother, who mourned her own loss in silence and kept her thoughts of grief private from the granddaughters who still reminded her too much of her own lost daughter. "She was a wonderful grandmother, but she was not a mother substitute," Mary explains. "She had this feeling that nothing could make up for her loss, that her tragedy was the biggest tragedy of all, and she never quite got the idea that maybe she should mother these motherless children, my sister and me."

Isolated and out of step with peers and grownups alike, Mary turned, instead, to her sister, who at fifteen became a kind of surrogate mother and whose fuller memories of their mother in her healthy years could help fill in the gaps. "But in spite of our closeness—and we remain close to this day—my sister had also lost her mother, and she had her own needs, too." So Mary continued to fantasize—at first, that her mother would indeed come back from some exotic journey to Africa, or that Mary herself would embark on a search and find her there.

Then, gradually, as the living image of "Mommy" receded into a dream image, the fantasy turned more into a motto, a wish, a "what if": "If only my mother were alive," she told herself, "then everything would be perfect!" And if that were the case, then where *was* Mommy? The question would torment her until she would think, in anger, "Where's Mommy! She's just not there when you need her!"

At the time of her mother's death, Mary felt the terrible but common anger and despair that Bowlby had observed. She went on a "search" in fantasy, as she would search later for the facts that would explain what had happened in reality. As she grew older, she came to feel the absence of her mother not only in her life but within her conception of herself and her identity, in ways similar to those described by Phyllis Silverman in her study.

"She wasn't there to answer my questions," Mary says. "Like: What kind of woman am I? What *is* it to be a woman

103

and a woman who will be attractive to men? Is it OK to be a career woman when my mother stayed home with my older sister and me? What kind of mother will I be? All these issues are intensified, and it's a struggle. You learn to be a mother by remembering how your mother was, but my memories are all truncated—the memories of a ten-year old."

Mary looks at the photograph again—the image frozen in time—and continues: "Now I'm no longer the child desperately wanting my mother. I'm an adult, also wondering what it was like for *her*—what kind of marriage *she* had, what was her relationship with *her* mother, and then what she felt at the end. I identify with her now as an adult. It feels good, it makes her feel more real.

"But we were deprived of knowing each other beyond a certain level. And you can never get around that. In some way, the person becomes a saint, with a saintly aura. You can never know her the way you know other people—what kinds of clothes did she wear, and what books did she read, what movies did she like, what foods did she eat? You lose the texture of the life. It's an experience that changes your life forever, and changes it at a time when you're extremely vulnerable. . . . " Mary's voice trails off, and I remember the words of my own father: "It changes your life forever. . . . "

"You learn to live with the scar tissue," she says at last. "You learn to live with it and accept it. You don't make excuses. It's your life."

"After the first death, there is no other." My first talk with Mary had taken place shortly before what turned out to be another cycle of loss: first, her divorce from her husband of four years, and then the death of her father. When we met for a second interview, on a bright December afternoon three years later, Mary gestured and spoke with the same determined vigor as before. She looked the same, only her hair was shorter, and the setting was different: Playing the gracious hostess in the new studio apartment that, she acknowledged with a shrug of the shoulders, felt oddly empty, she offered wine, cheese, and crackers, and answered my first question with a quick downward nod of the head.

"Would I be comfortable talking to you about the breakup of my marriage? No. But there was no question that all the losses played a role. A need for security. And there would be times when there would be real anger and frustration and a sense of his saying, 'I'm sick of hearing about all this!'

" . . . But Daddy's death . . . it made me realize the enormity of what I never had with my mother. I knew him as well as I would ever know him, and there are things that I will still miss—I hope to have a child, and if I do, Daddy will never know that child, and that will be hard. But I'll never have to wonder who, really, was my father. I really knew him.

"You know, it's just a totally different country, a nine-year-old and a thirty-three-year-old. It's all the difference in the world! My father's death came at a point in my life where there could be some closure. I mean, not only did I not get to know my mother as a teenager, but not in the early twenties and late twenties, when you are finding yourself. Yes, I'm very grateful that this came much later.

"And though we never had a conversation about this, my sister and I just knew that we were going to handle things differently from when Mommy died. We wanted to hear everything the doctor had to say, everything that was happening, and there was very much a sense of having a chance to say goodbye. We also arranged a lovely memorial service, at which people spoke, and my sister printed up all the speeches in a pamphlet and mailed it to everyone who attended. There are memories of things we did together all over this city, it helps me feel connected to him. . . .

"Yes, I feel very connected to him," she concludes. "But when both your parents die, there's no one between you and mortality anymore. I think that's the impression that I'm left with the most."

She pauses, looks away, looks at her watch, and then reminds me that an old friend is stopping by in a few minutes . . . It is a way of saying that it is time to push all this past behind her now and return to the day-to-day business of her present life. Yet, as Mary spoke, she also clearly enjoyed the act of remembering, showing me photographs of the husky, cigar-smoking man embracing the grown daughter who was still his baby. Perhaps, she was saying, the past and the present can coexist, after all.

"There's a sort of a melancholy that comes over me sometimes, a pervasive sadness, and I get fed up with it: will it never go away?"

Jocelyn* is an orphan, she tells me—but as a woman in her early fifties, she laughs nervously at a word that conjures up the image of a sad young waif. I also laugh, for the underlying sadness that she describes is not at all apparent in her buoyant smile.

She is a petite woman with a pixie haircut—light-brown hair with bangs, overshadowing bright blue eyes that seem never to look away from you. Certainly, they do not blink as she tells you the story of her parents' sudden deaths when she was three.

The gentle lilt to her alto voice is understated, without pretension. So is the way she dresses—a stylishly casual skirt and sweater in neutral colors. But if Jocelyn's manner is subdued, her apartment—overlooking the vast greenery of Manhattan's Central Park—gives a different impression. It is painted bright green and burgundy, and the walls are like gallery walls, covered with abstract art—haunting images in black and white by contemporary American artists. It is an incongruously beautiful setting in which to hear Jocelyn's story. Yet as she shows each print, then tells her tale, her tone changes little, as if to say, These are the artworks on the wall, these are the facts of my life, but there is this difference: I cannot choose the facts of my life, and I do not wish to display them. However, if you ask, I will tell you, and I will not look away. I will look at you—look at my life—in the same unblinking way that the prints stare at you from the walls.

"My father died first, very suddenly, of a cerebral hemorrhage," she begins, setting down a mug of coffee. "I was only three, and I remember vaguely his just collapsing and dying. And then, about six months later, my mother died. I don't remember her being unwell or anything—my memories are very, very vague.

"But the relevant thing is that nobody talked about it. My parents were never mentioned, it was a taboo subject. They just disappeared.

"And then my next major loss was when I was nine. That's when my grandmother died"—the grandmother who had taken her in at her parents' death. "I don't remember being very close to her or having any feeling about her. My grandmother was distant, wasn't affectionate—she was a very powerful and strong woman. I don't remember grieving for her.

"But I do remember the incredible fear and despair. Fear about what was going to happen to me. Fear. Uncertainty. A feeling of being terribly abandoned.

"Because I would overhear all the grown-up talk: My mother's sister had her hands full with four children of her own. And they didn't quite know what to do with me."

To Jocelyn, "they" were the entire world of grownups. Hers was a tiny, unheard voice against the din of grown-up talk; and even if they could hear her voice, what would she say?

She didn't speak; she cried. One day, a distant relative arrived in a car and took Jocelyn to what they told her would be her new home in a different city, two hundred miles away. "I don't think I stopped crying the whole time I was there. They only kept me two weeks, I was so distresed. . . . Then they brought me back to my aunt, who had found a couple in the neighborhood who had lost a daughter about my age and said they would see if I would fit in.

"And they were kind to me, this couple, and they became, as it were, my parents, and eventually my children's grandparents.

"But one of the things I was always very conscious of, that

is still a sadness to me, is that my real parents were never talked about. This couple were very keen for me to be their child, and I don't think it was particularly conscious on their part, but they didn't want any contact with my family or to talk about my parents. They didn't have to tell me not to talk about them, you just knew it was a taboo subject.

"So I knew very little. I don't have any photographs. Nothing. No stories about them. No history about them. . . .

"And I used to get sort of exhausted, not wanting to talk about my history, not wanting to explain that I had a foster mother instead of a mother. So I just started calling her mother instead of aunt, because I wanted to join in and be like everyone else."

The story continues: Jocelyn married young and had four children in quick succession. "I was trying to recreate in my own life what I hadn't had. I wanted so much to be part of a unity. It was to be my defense. I was going to be inside this kind of shell."

The shell was thick, but fears and fantasies penetrated, nonetheless: fears that burglars would enter the house, murder Jocelyn and her husband, and leave their children helpless, with no one to care for them. Or fears that, when her husband was delayed on a business trip, a fatal accident had occurred. A child coming home late might mean the same thing. "It was my own terrible fear of being abandoned. It was awful, awful. . . . "

Through the years, there have also been the periodic bouts with melancholy—"not clinical depression, just a sense of being down." It is the sense of not belonging—not knowing anyone at a party—or of being abandoned—seeing her children grow up and leave home—that invariably triggers these feelings, she says. And they all go back to this, she feels: "There's the sense, unconsciously, that parents shouldn't die and leave you, if you're any good. If you really were good, they wouldn't have died; and so you feel it's your fault. Because you know if you were a good child and really worthwhile, then people wouldn't leave you. . . .

"But I think that professionally, my history has also added something," she continues. "My work [as a hospice coordinator] isn't the most cheerful work in the world, but I don't feel scared by it in the way many people do. It's something that I can do, it's not something that frightens me. I know how valuable this is. And maybe I am working out my own loss. Maybe this is one way of repairing it. . . .

"Nothing in my life has been an accident," she concludes. For her, as for her listener, all the transformations in her life —from lost little girl to homemaker to hospice administrator —make perfect, metaphorical sense. Still, "all that old baggage that you cart around" is still there, she says. And she laughs nervously again, as the interview ends and she prepares to leave for her office and her next appointment, counseling the family of a young patient who is terminally ill.

———

"Would I talk to you for your book? Sure! I fit into almost all of your chapters!" Iris* laughs heartily over the telephone. "Come on out and visit anytime you want."

I had first spoken to Iris several months before, after she wrote in response to an article I had published on infertility. She and more friends than she cared to name were going through the same struggles, she had revealed in that letter. Could she reprint my article in the newsletter of her local infertility support group?

When I called to say yes, I discovered something more about Iris. Her struggle with infertility was not the first chapter in her history of loss, and those earlier losses had made this one that much harder.

"When I was twelve, my father had open-heart surgery and didn't make it," Iris tells me, tapping ash from her cigarette. Her tone is blunt and tender at the same time. She is a stocky five feet tall, with curly dark hair and large brown eyes that, as we speak, focus somewhere beyond me, beyond the confines of her suburban garden apartment, and beyond the present into the remembered past.

"He had to go to another city for the operation," she says, "and I remember overhearing a telephone conversation between my mother, who was with my father at the hospital, and my grandmother, who was taking care of us at home. And that is when I started to understand that there was a very good chance that my father would never come home from this trip.

"And the thing that got me was that I had not realized that he might never come home until he was already gone. I never accepted it, and I never wanted to, that he wasn't going to come back.

"And so after the telephone call came that he had died, it took me a long time to acknowledge that he was not coming home. I would sit up all night long. Because I would think, The truth is not that he has died, but that my parents are getting divorced. They made up this whole story so I wouldn't go with my father and leave my mother.

"So my mother would go to sleep, and I would get up and sit in the living room all night long, waiting for my father to come back for his things. Because if he did come back, I wanted to be there to say, 'Wait! I'm coming with you!'

"I did that for two years. And even after my mother closed up a suitcase with all his clothes to give away, I opened it up and took some of the stuff out, because I wanted him to have something to wear when he came home.

"My father would have been thirty-six that June. And instead of letting us stay at home that summer, my mother sent my younger sister and me away to camp. It was a horrendous summer. Came visiting day, and I thought, Why is only my mother visiting me? I thought, Everyone is looking at me, asking, 'Where's her father?'

"It wasn't until high school that I had a different kind of experience with that. In gym class one day, this girl turns to me and says, 'Listen, would you mind taking a drive with me to pick up my high school graduation pictures?' I said sure, but why? 'Oh, you wouldn't understand,' she keeps repeating whenever I ask. 'What do you mean I wouldn't understand?

110

Just tell me, all right?' Finally, my friend says, 'OK. My father died. This is a sad time for me. I don't want to pick up these pictures by myself.' Then I told her that I *did* understand. I had lost my father myself. She started to cry, and the things she told me, it was as if she were telling me my own story, including waiting up for her father to return. And we became very close friends, to this day.

"Well, a couple of years after my father died, my mother met my stepfather. He was a nice man, I had nothing against him, but at first I was a real bitch. My mother would say, 'Set the table,' and I would set it for three, instead of for four—as if he weren't there. But he never gave me a hard time about it; he must have understood that I wasn't at peace with my father's death yet, and eventually we became very close. I think it started when I was in the hospital, with mono, the summer I was sixteen. I thought, He's a nice guy, and he deserves better treatment. . . .

"My father and my stepfather weren't at all alike, but they became alike when my stepfather got sick. . . . I felt that I couldn't do anything for my father, it was too late. But I was going to make up for that with my stepfather. I wasn't working at the time that he had his stroke, and I would stay home with him all day to take care of him.

"When he got worse, we had to put him in the hospital. And on those visits, I would start to have flashbacks: Is this my father lying in bed, or my stepfather? Now, I had never seen my natural father in the hospital, I only had my imagination. But I would ask myself, when they were hooking up the oxygen, 'Is this how my father looked?'

"And as devastating as it might have been when I was twelve to see my father in the hospital, I think I would have been better off having seen him, rather than having to look at my stepfather all hooked up and say, 'My God! Is that what my father looked like?'

"So I lost two fathers," Iris says. "And as I watched my stepfather dying, I found myself reacting from twenty years before.

111

"At the cemetery, I felt that I was destined: I wasn't to have a father; I wasn't to be able to keep my stepfather. And I could not bear a child. I felt that my life was all death and emptiness, that I was being cruelly punished. I don't feel that way now, but I do feel I am entitled to a better time."

A better time. When I spoke to Iris, on a sultry September day, she was in the midst of struggling to find her way to that better time, pursuing an adoption. Throughout our interview, she was also fielding telephone calls from members of her infertility and adoptive parents support group.

I can't help but overhear these calls, and when I ask about her work—all volunteer, all unpaid—she shrugs. "Why am I so devoted to the group? It goes back to when I lost my father," she says, letting the word "father" stand for both lost fathers now. "Because I was alone, and nobody should have to be alone. Because when you walk into a room and see that twenty other people are having the same problem you are, that's where your strength comes from. Knowing that you aren't isolated. Knowing that you aren't alone."

———

Mary, Jocelyn, and Iris all searched for their lost parents in fantasy and memory and found themselves remembering them in different ways at different points in their lives. If one note comes through strongly in all their voices, it is that of determination: a determination to find ways to try to heal the wound, repair the damage, and go on with life, not as an embittered person but perhaps as a more knowing one. That note is similar to the one sounded by the child survivors whom Sarah Moskovitz interviewed as adults. It also can be heard in a poem I wrote after my mother's death when I was twenty-two:

First Rites
It was my mother initiated me.
Her dying, my first death,
Her kaddish had with me no precedent.

She loved me more than any child could bear,
And yet it fit somehow
That she who taught me
How to scale the world in octaves
Would plummet to a whisper's end,
Rasping,
"Survive." An omen
That I will. I will.

Rereading that poem now, I am struck by its love and anguish, but also by its presumption. I did not know that less than two years after my mother's death, I was to face what I thought would be my own.

4

LIVING
IN DOUBT

Being diagnosed with a fatal illness, surviving a traumatic accident, or living through catastrophe forces us to confront a loss like no other—the loss of ourselves. "Living in Doubt" was the title Peter had given to the memoir he wrote of his bout with cancer. "Seeing Things Through to the End" might have been the title for my mother's final journal, had she kept one. My title could be "Nobody Promised You Tomorrow," a phrase that has stayed with me from my own brush with death. Taken together, these mottoes suggest a double-sided image of personal vulnerability balanced by what may seem to an outsider like stubborn endurance but to the patient or victim feels more like business as usual, except that he may have just discovered, with heightened urgency, what the most important business in his own life is.

Both perspectives are common to those confronting their own end. One may live through the threat of death or imminent disaster, only to be left in its wake with the wreckage of one's most basic illusions about the nature of a safe, benign world. With old meanings shattered, we must develop new ones that can encompass painfully acquired knowledge about just how vulnerable life leaves us.[1]

Having seen both Peter and Mom through their struggles, I thought I had understood their accommodation with life and with death. But I had been the involved observer only, never the participant in these contests between life and death.

Then my turn came to face the possibility of my own extinction. On a bright March day thirteen years ago, Hanafi Muslim gunmen seized the B'nai B'rith Building in Washington, D.C., where I then worked, and held more than one hundred men and women hostage for thirty-nine hours. I was one of them.

The realization that the world would continue without me as it had before me was terrifying and humbling. The world I had learned to live in again after Mom's death seemed a dangerous place, yet I had also managed to find shelter in my new life with Peter. Now, suddenly, as gunmen threatened to chop off our heads with machetes, there was no safety at all. Still, I ultimately resolved, if somehow I managed to survive, I would seize what seemed a second chance at life, heal whatever wounds remained from my old life, and celebrate new joy.

During the hours of my captivity, discovering what my short life had meant became a need as urgent as food or water; afterward, fulfilling the promises I had made to myself in the time of crisis compelled me forward no less urgently. Yet this personal quest to discover meaning in the wake of crisis is

[1] "Generally, the single most common response to negative life events such as crime, disease, and accidents is an intense feeling of vulnerability," according to University of Massachusetts psychologist Ronnie Janoff-Bulman. See her paper, "Assumptive Worlds and the Stress of Traumatic Events: Applications of the Schema Construct," *Social Cognition*, July 1989, and book in press, *Shattered Assumptions* (New York: The Free Press, 1992).

Also see *Loss and Change*, by Peter Marris, and Viktor Frankl's *Man's Search for Meaning*. Marris and Frankl both discuss the search for new structure and meaning in the wake of different kinds of loss, including natural disaster and the confrontation with one's mortality.

also a universal one. It is what Viktor Frankl calls man's "will to meaning."

According to Frankl, the search for meaning is man's driving motivational force, even in the face of family tragedy, unavoidable suffering, or one's own imminent mortality. When meaning is lost, the will to live is lost, too: this was the essential lesson Frankl learned from his experience as an inmate at Auschwitz, Dachau, and other Nazi death camps. He described how fellow inmates who managed to conceive an inner goal or found some meaning to their suffering—whether it was the need to bear witness or the strength to suffer with dignity—were better able to endure what were surely unendurable conditions. This newfound meaning gave them the will to survive, Frankl asserted. But those who lost this will to meaning invariably also lost their will to live.

> Once an individual's search for a meaning is successful, it not only renders him happy but also gives him the capability to cope with suffering. And what happens if one's groping for a meaning has been in vain? This may well result in a fatal condition. Let us recall, for instance, what sometimes happened in extreme situations such as prisoner-of-war camps or concentration camps. In the first, as I was told by American soldiers, a behavior pattern crystallized to which they referred as 'give-up-itis.' In the concentration camps, this behavior was paralleled by those who one morning, at five, refused to get up and go to work and instead stayed in the hut, on the straw wet with urine and feces. Nothing—neither warnings nor threats—could induce them to change their minds. And then something typical occurred: they took out a cigarette from deep down in a pocket where they had hidden it and started smoking. At that moment we knew that for the next forty-eight hours or so we would watch them dying.[2]

For those suffering from chronic or fatal illness, the discovery of new meaning can have a similarly powerful impact—

[2] *Man's Search for Meaning*, 141.

perhaps not adding days to a life that is ending but certainly adding dignity and meaning to the life that remains. Erik Erikson described a somewhat similar struggle to live through the last stage of the life cycle, that of old age, with a sense of integrity, wisdom, and hope, rather than feelings of disdain and despair. It seems to me that this is the conflict faced whenever death looms, however old or young one is. I think of my mother, at fifty-seven, suffering from terminal cancer, "willing" herself to live to see her children established and her ailing parents and sister taken care of— willing herself, finally, to die in dignity, at home, as she had chosen. I think of Peter, in his early twenties, battling his cancer, willing himself back to life even as he wrote his memoir.

The meaning or purpose that is found will differ for every individual. Thus, for Mom, facing illness carried one meaning, while for Peter, learning to live in doubt and with hope carried another.

Here is another example: For Peter Noll, a contemporary Swiss legal scholar, professor, and author, who set down his reflections on his final year in his posthumously published journal, *In the Face of Death*, the question posed by his struggle with terminal cancer was: "*What* wisdom does thinking about death impart?" Time itself, for one thing, he reflected, "becomes all the more important the clearer we know its boundary." The experience of doing even mundane things also changed in an unexpected way: "Seeing something for the last time is nearly as good as seeing it the first time," Noll commented suggestively. Relationships with others also differed, as Noll realized with the only regret voiced throughout his brave journal, for he had little time left to follow his own advice: "Love those more who love you; devote yourself less to those who don't love you."[3]

As Noll noted, we tend to call such reflections wisdom. Erikson also cited wisdom as one of the hallmarks of old age

[3] Peter Noll, *In the Face of Death* (New York: Viking, 1989).

at the approach of death, defining it as an "informed and detached concern with life itself in the face of death itself."[4]

Yet these new meanings and the changed perspective through which life is seen do not spring up full-blown within the patient or accident victim. They arise as part of a longer internal process, one described in detail by Elisabeth Kübler-Ross. Although she based her theories on her work with terminal cancer patients, they are relevant to anyone facing death from any cause. For instance, I recognized many of the emotional states and attitudes delineated in her work in my own experience as a hostage, while I observed others in both Peter and my mother during their respective illnesses.

I recognized many but not all, for each person's passage is unique. Kübler-Ross put forth five stages through which the dying person passes: denial and isolation; anger; bargaining; depression; and, finally, acceptance. Whether you call them "stages," phases, or emotional states, however, Kübler-Ross emphasizes that they can occur in a confused jumble that follows no particular order, with some feelings passing quickly, only to recur unpredictably, then fading and appearing once more.

When I was held hostage, for instance, at first I felt all the numbness, shock, and horror Kübler-Ross described as belonging to her first stage, and only by denying and detaching myself from reality through fantasy and various other mental tricks (which also resembled the inner mechanisms she described) was I able to cope with my fears. However, all these feelings and stratagems of denial coexisted with depression throughout my captivity and would for periods of time disappear, then recur, and disappear again. Thus, rather than manifesting themselves as two separate, consecutive stages, denial and anger were tangled together throughout.

The denial stage also followed no set order during either Peter's bout with cancer or my mother's final illness. In fact,

[4] Erik Erikson, *The Life Cycle Completed* (New York: Norton, 1982), 61.

Peter and I turned most to mutual denial and deception only some time after the operation—when, even though his radiation treatments had left him virtually unable to talk, we "spoke" nightly on the telephone. Similarly, during Mom's final illness, depression and acceptance continually lived side by side with denial. And it was this very insistence on going about the daily business of living that allowed her (and me) to focus on the many small pleasures of life that were left to her.

Anger, too, came at different times and took different forms: For me, it poured out only after I was released from captivity. For Mom, depression came first and lingered as an underlying sadness throughout her last year, and only at the very close of her life did she, always so soft-spoken, begin to express a quiet outrage at past indignities that she would tolerate no more. For his part, Peter expressed no anger at all (even refusing to ask "Why me?") until after he was well on the way to recuperating, at which point a hazy irritability settled over him for a time.

I also suppose it could have been called bargaining—the stage in which the person facing death essentially makes a promise, bet, or bargain with God in order to postpone the inevitable—when I inwardly resolved, "If I live, I shall make something good happen out of all this." And perhaps it was a similar kind of bargaining that led Mom to wish to see her children launched and to leave with her life in good order.

But my resolution as a hostage was far more than bargaining; it was a crucial part of the much larger process of finding meaning even in a life that seemed to be coming to an early, violent end. Further, it was only when I reached this wider perspective that I could then feel within something like Kübler-Ross's concept of acceptance. Similarly, Mom may have "bargained" with God to allow her to do what she felt she must; but more important, those goals also provided meaning to that last year and, in doing so, perhaps prolonged life itself. Was this "bargaining," "acceptance"—or something more?

To me, the very word "acceptance" connotes passivity

rather than the real internal struggles that precede what many psychologists prefer to call accommodation or adaptation. What matters more than words, however, is that one can indeed develop a different view of the life that came before, as well as whatever life remains or comes next. And this vision can illuminate what you see with new and different meaning: Your life will be a new life, seen as if for the first time.

———

Imagine that you are sitting in your office one bright spring morning, sipping a cup of tea. From the open window, a breeze tickles the back of your neck. You listen to the noise of the city and dream of a Haydn string quartet. On the way to work, you have smelled, then glimpsed, the first yellow sprigs of the season. It is March in Washington, when sun and sky and pale green leaves tease you with thoughts of summer, and you begin each day wondering if this is the day that the cherry blossoms will suddenly cover the Potomac's shores like tiny pink parasols.

Now the breeze tickles your neck again, and you hear a sound that might be gunshots, but you know it is only a car backfiring, three, four, five times, a distant popping. Then there is silence, and you don't think about how unusually quiet it is for a busy downtown street, until you answer the phone and hear a colleague from down the hall whisper, "There are gunmen in the building. Barricade yourself in your office. Watch out."

This is not a fantasy. This is what happened on the morning of March 9, 1977, as I sat in my office on the eighth floor of the B'nai B'rith Building in downtown Washington, where I had moved just a year and a half before, shortly after my mother's death. Only weeks earlier, I had walked into work one morning with a sense of peace and contentment I had not felt since before Peter's illness. It must have showed, for a colleague stopped me at the elevator to exclaim, "You look great, Diane! You look"—she paused, and then continued—

"happy." I smiled and thought that perhaps my seasons of mourning had ended at last.

I worked as the assistant editor of the *National Jewish Monthly*, and as I went about my job that morning, awaiting the arrival of the final proof of the next issue of the magazine, there was no hint that I, along with more than one hundred of my colleagues, was about to become something more and less than human: hostage to an armed group of terrorists.

I heard the shouting first—fierce, gruff, filled with obscenities. I froze, dazed, until my boss and another colleague came into my office, locked the door, and shoved my desk against it. But within seconds the door was splintering under the pressure of a rifle butt. And the voices, the obscenities, continued.

It had the surreal feel and sound of a nightmare, but one at once so outlandish and real that you could not be dreaming. When the door flew open, we saw a black man in his early twenties, neatly dressed in blue jeans and a brown leather jacket, pointing a rifle at us. He jabbed the butt of his gun in my boss's face at the bridge of his nose. I heard a startled cry of pain and the tinkle of eyeglasses falling to the floor.

Now a second gunman appeared. Like the first, he was neatly groomed, with a trim mustache, and he wore blue jeans and a leather jacket. Instead of a rifle, however, he carried a revolver, and from the steel chain belted around his waist hung a machete.

A machete? The blade was bright, but my mind felt dull, stunned, as unable to make sense of what was happening as were the half-dozen or so office friends and colleagues who I now saw had also been rounded up. I looked at these well-known faces, colleagues at work, now colleagues in captivity, and assumed their blank eyes were a reflection of my own. Then I heard the distant, muffled sound of footsteps coming toward us, and I knew there would be still more gunmen, still more hostages.

The gunmen prodded us into a large, empty room that was being renovated—the conference room, a low-ceilinged, cavernous space located on the same floor as my office. Cans of paint and plaster lay open on the concrete floor, filling the air with the faintly nauseating smell of glue and turpentine. There we stood in uneven rows and grimly watched the macabre procession of more gunmen and more hostages into the room.

Still standing, we were made to count off: the numbers stopped at around one hundred. The sight of smeared, dried blood on so many of my colleagues' faces, the sound of muffled sighs, and the sour odor of sweat and fear, which was already overtaking the smell of the paint, combined to make my head and stomach spin with a giddy lightness that went past nausea. In the row beside me stood a woman with whom I had once worked closely, the daughter of an Orthodox rabbi. "Hold my hand," I whispered, pleading, "Give me some of your faith." She squeezed tightly, and the grasp of her hand conveyed something like hope.

Then, limp, moaning, and soaked with blood, a man was carried into the room by his arms and legs. His pants and shirt were a mass of red; a makeshift tourniquet was wrapped around his thigh. I recognized him immediately as an easygoing, good-humored young man in his early twenties. He was a member of the moving crew who had been helping with office renovations since the fall, and now he lay on the floor, already only semi-conscious, perhaps dying. Fortunately, one of the other hostages had known enough first aid to put on the makeshift tourniquet that was keeping him alive. Even more fortunately, the gunmen listened to her brave, persistent pleas to allow him to be taken to a hospital.

Perhaps, I thought, this small mercy would be an omen of further mercies, even though at the moment none seemed likely. I had counted six gunmen so far and guessed that others must be stationed throughout the building. Already they had threatened us with rifles, shotguns, pistols, machetes, knives, and an ornamentally sheathed sword.

I gazed around me and saw that many of my colleagues' faces were fierce with anger. But with no weapons of our own, we were helpless, powerless. Anyone who dared to act the "hero," our captors warned with the wave of a rifle or a sword, would endanger us all. They had threatened us even as they bound the men's hands with electrical wire. Then the gunmen had ordered us to lie down on the cold, dusty floor— the women on one side of the room, the men on the other— and we had no choice but to comply.

As we lay there, I found myself listening to the bright chiming of bells from two nearby churches. They rang every fifteen minutes, one minute apart, as if to confirm that we had made it through another quarter of an hour. Instinctively, I wound my watch, affirming that time would continue, and so would I. But as the litany of our captors' threats continued, no occupation was available except to count these dragging minutes, to pray, to watch for the smallest signs of hope, and to worry about fates over which we no longer had control.

Finally, a thickset man in his fifties, dressed dramatically in black and with a trim pepper-and-salt goatee, strode boldly through the room. Older than the other gunmen and clearly in command, he wore strapped around his waist a machete that swung slowly back and forth like the sword of Damocles.

"Do any of you remember the murder of the family of Hamaas Abdul Khaalis by Black Muslim gunmen?" he demanded. "They slew my babies. They shot my wife. I want revenge." Thus did Hamaas Abdul Khaalis introduce himself.

Dimly, I recalled the case: Four years before, gunmen had brutally murdered six members of Khaalis's family—five of his children and his nine-day-old grandson.

But the murderers of his family were still alive, Khaalis went on. They had gone to prison, but they had not been sentenced to death, for there was no death penalty in the District of Columbia. Now, Khaalis declared, justice must prevail: The convicted murderers of his children must be given over to the custody of Khaalis and the group he headed, the Hanafi Muslims. Then Khaalis and his men would mete out their own justice.

At the same time, Khaalis said, the recently released movie

Mohammad, Messenger of God must be closed. It defamed the life and message of the founder of Islam, and such blasphemy could not be tolerated.

If these demands were not met, Khaalis promised, "Heads will roll! We'll chop your heads off and throw them out the windows!"

He pointed a gun at individual hostages: "Do you doubt that there are men who are not afraid to die for their faith? That there are men who will live by their faith and will die for it, by the sword? . . . For every man of mine that is hurt, I will kill ten of you."

I did not dare to doubt, even as I listened with utter bafflement while Khaalis raged not only against his family's murderers but against the government, against the movies, and most of all against the Jewish people. Here was a man who had suffered the most shocking tragedy imaginable—the murder of his family—and for that he deserved the deepest sympathy. But no one at the B'nai B'rith Building bore even the remotest relation to his tragedy, possessed even the smallest power to meet his demands. The nightmare had become a waking terror that rested on a logic I could not penetrate. There was nothing to do but wait in an agony of uncertainty, with the very real sword of Khaalis dangling above our heads.

How do you endure the threat of death not just physically but mentally? How do you continue to live, knowing that you might die? Is it possible to discover some new meaning or new sense of one's identity even in a life's last months, days, or minutes, and if so, how does it happen? What are the mental strategies and the mental processes by which one manages to arrive at this new meaning, even under the most dire circumstances?

Elisabeth Kübler-Ross described the stages leading to acknowledgment and acceptance among terminal cancer patients. More recently, Mardi J. Horowitz, a psychiatrist and

124

professor at the University of California, has proposed a somewhat similar series of phases for people whose lives have been threatened. In his view, survivors of disaster generally go through an initial period of stunned fear, sadness, and rage, which he has termed outcry. Then comes denial, then a time in which intrusive, unbidden thoughts of what happened cannot be stopped. These stages alternate and overlap and are felt differently by every individual. But eventually comes a period of "working through" and "completion," in which life goes on once more—but not unchanged.

University of Massachusetts psychologist Ronnie Janoff-Bulman posited a somewhat similar process, at the conclusion of which something very like what Viktor Frankl had described years before also takes place: After one's assumptions of a safe, invulnerable world have been shaken by disaster or the threat of death, new meanings and assumptions gradually will be rebuilt in their stead. If they are not, long-term difficulties may arise. The challenge is not to "get over" disaster but to find a new way to go on.

As a hostage, I knew nothing of these theories or research findings. But what happened to me in the course of the thirty-nine hours of my captivity and in its aftermath during the weeks, months, and years that followed urged me forward to a new definition of myself.

I am skeptical of psychics, suspicious of new-age spirituality. Yet throughout those thirty-nine hours of captivity I felt myself existing on several planes at once. In retrospect, I also see the larger outlines of a process by which I came to see my second life with a new vision of who I was and would be.

Outwardly, I obeyed every command by Khaalis and his gunmen to listen and be silent, to stand or lie down. I cringed at each new threat to chop off our heads, jumped with fear when a gun fired suddenly in the middle of the night. In this sense, I was like a dog in a Pavlovian experiment: terror was the stimulus, and I submitted and was trained.

Inwardly, however, a different process was at work—one

so darkly interior that even now I find it difficult to explain. It had to do with hope and something like faith, and an inner struggle to find some way to fight back, however silent and invisible my way might be to everyone but me. Finally, it was an urgent journey of discovery, where my time was short but my goal must be met—to uncover some meaning in everything that had come before and whatever it was that might happen next.

This process began with the simple realization that I must find some way to remain calm. The various mental tricks and games that succeeded in quieting my trembling, however, gradually transported me into a heightened meditative state in which all the unanswered questions of my life were seen to possess simple solutions, if only I could live to fulfill them. If I could somehow manage to survive, I resolved, I would find a way to make something good come out of all this, and I would build a new life—with Peter, with my family, and with myself.

But all these thoughts were as yet hazy, unformed clouds as I lay on the dusty concrete floor beside a colleague who was also a friend. Too frightened to cry, she rocked silently in place, her skin chalky white—as I must have looked when, earlier, another friend had given me hope. Now it was my turn to pass along the strength that others had passed to me.

I gently murmured, "Shh! Shh!" and stroked her hair. I whispered, "It's hard, but try to think about something else. If you think about missing your husband or what *might* happen, you'll just go crazy. Think about something else, think about *anything* else. . . . Calm down. . . . Calm down. . . . "

She grew quiet, and so did I, and I realized that in comforting her, I was comforting myself. Moreover, the very act of helping somehow soothed. And I remember thinking that perhaps, even in the most terrifying circumstances, it was possible to make a difference, however small, to someone.

Until then, my primary focus had been to search for hope amid every move and gesture by our captors. For instance, the fact that Khaalis had asked for telephones from the start indicated that though we remained sealed from the world's view, at least there was some communication with that unseen world—a world we might yet see again.

Another small reason to hope: Along with all the guns and ammunition that Khaalis and his men had hauled into the conference room, they had brought large yellow jars of apple juice and white Styrofoam cups. Food was sustenance—not only for the gunmen but, I prayed, eventually for us too.

But so intense a focus not only magnified each small hope; it heightened and exaggerated very real fears: What if the telephone lines were cut? What if a deadline *was* set? What if the gunmen already had emptied their coffee cups and jars of apple juice and could wait no longer?

Such busy thoughts, I began to see, led straight to fear and trembling. Could I somehow replace them with other thoughts?

During Peter's illness and Mom's, I had learned that detachment, like denial, is a way of knowing and not knowing. As I faced the possibility of my own death, I saw that distancing myself from what might happen, through fantasy or sheer suppression of reality, also provided a way to escape momentarily the fate over which I had no control.

I began by telling myself that if my time had come, then it had come. Perhaps if I repeated that message often enough, I would even come to believe it. I used gallows humor, telling myself that if I lived to remember these hours, certainly I would never forget them; and that, though Dostoyevsky had faced the czar's firing squad, it was not at all necessary for every aspiring writer to have such an experience.

I laughed under my breath, but it was a hollow laugh. My pulse and brain were still racing. Hard as I tried, I was not a very convincing stoic. What other strategies could I find?

"Calm down," I had told my friend. Now I repeated the words for my own benefit, again and again, in imitation of the mantras and yoga exercises I had heard so many friends extol but at which, until that moment, I had scoffed: "Calm down. . . . Calm down. . . . Calm down. . . . "

"Calm down," echoed some inner voice, now no longer my own. "Your worrying won't help you get out of here, so what good will it do, however much you worry? If you must concentrate on something, then concentrate on music—on practicing your flute." I had so little time, and yet so much time, what else was there to do? In preparation for some future flute lesson that I now might never take, inwardly I played through Bach, Handel, Devienne. And as I played the notes —slowly, carefully, with more feeling than I had ever managed in reality—the mournful melodies lulled me into a new reflective mood.

There, in that sleepy state midway between tranquillity and terror, my thoughts turned more deeply inward still. I remembered how, though my mother knew she was dying, at the same time she had continued to hope that some miracle cure or drug might yet save her. Whenever Mom voiced these thoughts, I had taken her hand to help ward off what I took to be sheer terror. Only now did I understand that perhaps it took the greatest courage of all to hope when there was no hope left.

If only I could tell her that—that and so much more. And suddenly, in this crisis that had placed me so close to death and by extension so close to where she was now, I conjured her presence within and inwardly poured out to her all my regrets—about her, about Peter, about all the now never-to-be-fulfilled dreams that she had dreamed for me and that I had dreamed for myself. Yet soon I would be with her once more. I would be with her, and all our unfinished conversations would continue forever. . . . Already, I had begun to feel my mother's warm embrace, and the thought of her touch brought comfort.

Then another, different voice within reminded me of how many words I had also left unsaid to Peter, to my father, and to my brothers. So many things remained undone, and I regretted most of all that I had not had time to marry Peter.

Well, there had been reasons, I told myself: After Mom's death, Dad had maintained objections to Peter, chiefly relating to Peter's uncertain health, and I was not ready for a struggle that threatened to estrange me from the one parent I had left. Peter and I had waited; now I saw with more sadness than I could bear that we had waited too long. If only I could tell *him* that. . . . I looked about desperately for a pencil, a piece of paper—anything on which to scratch some final loving message for Peter, even just a chalk mark on the dusty floor.

I had willed myself to be calm, but now, replaying in memory all his endearments that I would never hear again, I could not be calm. I fled instead into a final, desperate fantasy of denial and escape.

I dreamed now that I was actually two people—a real Diane and this dream one: for surely it was only some peculiar trick of the imagination that had set me on this bare concrete floor awaiting death.

In fact, the "real" Diane had called in sick this morning. In fact, at that very moment she was sitting at home with Peter, listening intently to every detail of the ordeal as it was reported on the radio. This Diane was fine; she will always be fine. She will live and marry Peter, and they will live happily ever after. . . .

But even as I dreamed of this parallel life, I knew that try as I might, I had outgrown such fairy tales forever. I had come full circle on my journey—from an initial sense of walking through a waking nightmare to a still more vivid knowledge that no dream, however vivid, would protect me. Nor had any stigma marked me for special punishment. And however far or deep was the journey I took in imagination, it could never secure a final escape from the very real terrors that life may hold.

"Nobody promised you tomorrow," Khaalis had declared to us, his captives, with the boldness of a god. And I thought of the "promise" that young lives are supposed to have, and that my life would end empty of any fulfillment at all.

At that moment I remembered a favorite Jewish proverb: "If you save one person's life, it is as if you have saved the world." I thought of how I had struggled to save both Peter and Mom, how hard I had tried to make a difference to Mom during her last year, and how lovingly I had cared for Peter. And now, even as we all faced the possibility of death, small acts of kindness had helped me, and I had tried to help others in turn. Now I repeated another Jewish saying: "Be strong, be strong, and let us strengthen one another." Yes, we had made one another stronger, and we had made a difference to each other, and perhaps that was enough.

I looked up from the floor where we all had been told to lie and tried to peer out the high row of windows. Very early on the first day there, the gunmen had ordered several hostages to paint over the windows so that no police could peer in. The beige-brown smears had long since dried, turning the color of excrement.

But the next morning's light could be detected dimly, even so. Another day was passing, the Red Cross had been allowed to send in juice and coffee and fruit, and Khaalis had told us, "Pray to whoever you pray to. Even if you pray to a tree, pray to that." I had prayed, and I had passed beyond prayer, and I now knew what it meant to make peace with one's life.

Then that day, too, passed, until a total of thirty-nine hours had gone by, and finally the gunmen ordered us to close our eyes, keep silence, freeze. It was in that silent darkness that, according to an agreement about which we hostages knew nothing, the gunmen left and in their place the police arrived to restore our freedom.

One of the rabbis who had been held captive led us in the traditional Jewish prayer: "Blessed art Thou, O Lord our God, King of the Universe, who has kept us in life, and hast preserved us, and enabled us to reach this season."

"Amen," we said. It was three o'clock in the morning, and the world outside was dark. But we had reached this season, and we were free.

———

"Nobody promised you tomorrow," Khaalis had declared. But after so much trembling and fear, I resolved, there would also be joy. There must be joy—and with it, a renewal, both physical and spiritual.

For the moment, I still hovered between two worlds—the nightmare from which I had just emerged and the giddy heights from which I surveyed what could only seem a second chance at life. It was a chance I resolved to seize—I would marry Peter and heal old wounds with my family and with myself.

When I returned to our apartment, every color, texture, smell, and taste was discovered anew, with a newborn infant's joy—Peter's soothing touch, the fresh smell of clean sheets, the sweet and tangy taste of a fresh orange. A long, hot shower became a baptism of sorts in which I cleansed myself of the gritty film from the dusty floor, though I knew that mere water could not wash away the terror I had felt. Then, huddled peacefully in Peter's arms, I fitfully started awake from each new dream, fearing what visions I might see, until I remembered Peter's first words to me upon my return: "Let's get married right away before something else happens!" And how, just as emphatically, I had said yes.

Later, seized by restlessness, I stepped outside and, holding Peter's hand, felt a fresh March breeze brush against my cheeks. "Look at me!" I wanted to call out to every stranger who passed by. "I'm alive! Alive, after all."

It was a cry I felt like shouting all along the highway as we drove to Baltimore, to my father's house, where my family had decorated the entryway with a banner that read: "Welcome home, Diane!" We would celebrate that welcome home together as a family—as a real family, I felt, for the first time since my mother's death. "Nobody promised you tomorrow," Khaalis had told us. But now that day was here, and it was a day for rejoicing.

Yet with this second life also came a sense of dread. For weeks, I would wake, shuddering, from nightmare visions of myself running, trapped by unknown persecutors dressed in black and wielding long knives that flashed in the sun. They would point guns and shout, "We're going to kill you!" Then noises would explode.

It would be months before I dreamed one final dream, that before those shots could ring out I had indeed escaped. But in the meantime the sound of footsteps tapping behind me, the sudden backfire of a car, even silence—almost anything out of the ordinary could renew the terror I so longed to quell, and transport me into a momentary state of fright and certain expectation of disaster.

Although various mental tricks had helped get me through the siege, now, as I learned additional details from the news accounts and listened to Peter and my family speak of their own ordeal of helpless waiting, the siege came to seem more frightening still in retrospect. Not just the B'nai B'rith Building had been seized, I discovered, but a floor of City Hall and Washington's Islamic Mosque. In all, one hundred thirty-one people had been taken hostage. Moreover, at City Hall, a young reporter had died of gunshot wounds. Another man there had suffered a fatal heart attack. I knew how close the young moving man in our own building had come to death. How close we had all come.

I grappled with these and other ghosts as I returned to work in the building where I had almost died. On my first trip back, I stood transfixed before the wreckage of what had been my office—the splinters, overturned furniture, reams of crumpled paper. How could you possibly "put the past behind you," as one friend counseled me, if you had to walk right back into it every morning at 9:00 A.M.?

These sorts of responses—ranging from nightmares to panic attacks to unbidden, intrusive thoughts to complete denial—haunted many of us who had lived through the hostage-taking. They characterize the syndrome commonly called post-traumatic stress disorder. Although most people think of post-traumatic stress syndrome as the inner wound left by the Vietnam War on the soldiers who served there, it is also a common aftermath to catastrophe, violent accidents, or the sudden confrontation with death.[5]

---

[5] See Mardi J. Horowitz, *Stress Response Syndromes* (New York: Jason Aronson, 1976). Also see Janoff-Bulman.

Wisely, B'nai B'rith began offering free group therapy sessions run by psychologists from George Washington University Hospital. Confidentiality was assured, but though a number of women took advantage of this opportunity to air our feelings, few men did. "We have to save face; only women attend that sort of thing," one man admitted in private.

Had he attended, he would have learned that the occasional attacks of fear and panic he felt were shared by others; that he was not alone in suffering from nightmares; and that others, too, were seeking ways to change their lives for good. I would marry Peter; another woman and her husband decided to start trying to have a child soon; still others planned to take much-needed vacations or simply to spend more time with their families.

He also would have heard sudden bursts of anger: understandable fury at the gunmen who had held us hostage, but also more irrational rage at colleagues who had not been in the building at the time and thus escaped being held hostage; anger at friends or family members who weren't responsive enough—or were perhaps too responsive, too protective; anger at everyone, and most especially at a world that was no longer and would never again be safe.

Such universal, unspecified anger is a common early response to any loss: *Why* were we subjected to this ordeal? *Who* was at fault for allowing this to happen? Erich Lindemann had described the rage, hostility, and need to blame villains among the survivors of the Coconut Grove fire in his 1944 paper. Many years later, as he faced his own terminal illness, Lindemann noted that the person who grieves his own loss must go through this stage of blaming, accusing, and finding fault as well.[6]

But in the same way that even paranoids can have enemies, some of this anger was justified. Soon after the siege, for instance, the magazine *Commentary* published an article that

---

[6] See "Reactions to One's Own Fatal Illness," in Erich Lindemann, *Beyond Grief: Studies in Crisis Intervention* (Northvale, N.J.: Jason Aronson, 1979).

enraged me. Its writer blamed us for being too passive and falling prey to the so-called Stockholm Syndrome, a peculiar phenomenon by which hostages begin to identify with their captors. The writer had not bothered to interview any of us. To my mind, she had distorted quotes and facts from other news reports to fit a preconceived polemic. Furious, I wrote a lengthy letter to the editor as a way of setting the record straight. I quote most of it below, both to show just how angry I was and to answer one of the most frequent (and irritating) questions I still hear when I mention to a new acquaintance that I was once held hostage: "Did you suffer from the Stockholm Syndrome?"

. . . Whereas the identification-with-the-aggressor syndrome relies on close personal contact and prolonged dialogue between the perpetrators of the terrorist act and their victims, in the B'nai B'rith building hostages were not allowed to speak, converse, or ask any questions of their captors. All such attempts were either disregarded or met with threats of violence: we were not to question, only to listen. And what we listened to were, for the most part, threats against our lives and attacks on the Jewish people.

Furthermore, the quotations Miss [Dorothy] Rabinowitz cites as expressing sympathy and compassion for Khaalis and the other Hanafis were taken out of context from newspaper accounts which appeared in the days immediately following the release of the hostages. Miss Rabinowitz herself acknowledges, near the end of her article, that at such a time feelings of gratitude for not having endured the final brutality—of murder itself—might overwhelm simultaneous feelings of anger, hostility, and fear. But the "peculiar nature" of these quotations has to do with more than just the time at which they were given. Is it not possible to respond to terrifying incidents with more complexity and subtlety than Miss Rabinowitz is willing to acknowledge? Is it not possible to feel compassion for someone who has lived through the brutal murders of members of his immediate family and at the same time to feel anger and hatred toward this same person for shooting at colleagues and threatening to cut off heads? Is it not further possible that, in facing what we thought was certain mass death, we sought to understand (and still do) the matrix of history that brought us to the point of those Hanafi guns?

Miss Rabinowitz seems not to have bothered to talk to any of the hostages in person or to have picked up any recent edition of the Washington *Post*, which daily has reported the testimony of some sixteen ex-hostages from the B'nai B'rith building against their former captors. Can this participation in the trial, as witnesses for the prosecution, be considered by any stretch of the imagination as a "collaboration" with our former captors or as serving "the further dissemination of the terrorists' "message"?

The absurdity—even the perversity—of Miss Rabinowitz's argument is further evidenced by her quoting one hostage as saying that the only people she "feared" were the police upon their arrival in the building. The fact is that at the moment of liberation the hostages were expecting gunfire, and so when the most unexpected event of all occurred—the arrival of our liberators, the police—there was at first shock and confusion. But almost immediately that "fear" that something still worse was to happen to us was transformed into great joy and jubilation. Hostages hugged the police, shook their hands, thanked them profusely. As a matter of record, B'nai B'rith gave Washington's police chief, Maurice J. Cullinane, a special humanitarian award at a public convocation of thanksgiving. In fact, this award was personally presented to Police Chief Cullinane by one of the ex-hostages.

Miss Rabinowitz accuses the majority of the nation's newspapers and magazines of being staffed by "that special society of editorial writers and 'advocacy' journalists whose business it is to serve as the nation's liberal conscience." I lack confidence in both the conscience and the consciousness of the author of such wrong-headed observations. The conscience of the B'nai B'rith hostages is clear.[7]

[7] My letter appeared in *Commentary* in August 1977, 7–8.

The siege continued to plague me in other ways as well. Besides suffering nightmares and sudden fears, I found myself adopting peculiar superstitions, as if magic alone would protect me in a world that promised no protection. For instance, because I had overslept and not had time to wash my hair the morning of the siege, I determined that I would never oversleep, never miss washing my hair again.

Similarly, many people immediately threw away the clothes they had worn on the day of the siege. Yet I clung to the cable-knit beige sweater I had worn that day—a final gift from my mother and one I cherished even more after the siege as possessing her special protective magic.

Luck often breeds superstition. It also can strengthen faith or weaken it. Although the siege neither shook nor confirmed the religious beliefs with which I had wrestled since high school, being held hostage helped crystallize my identity as a Jew as perhaps no other event could. For as I listened to our captors revile us with one vicious anti-Jewish tirade after another, thoughts of the Holocaust were inescapable.

Further, because we already had been separated according to gender, I worried that we might be divided next according to religion, and then who knew what would happen? Fortunately, this eventuality never came to pass, but in my uncertainty I found myself toying with the idea of lying about my real identity. After all, I did not "look" Jewish, nor was my name Jewish, and if I lied I probably could "pass" as a gentile. This stratagem seemed to offer a possible escape route, yet I was not comfortable with it. From childhood on and especially throughout the long hours of captivity, I had found comfort in the wisdom of rabbinic sayings and in a well-known passage from the Bible that later became a fitting epigraph for my "second" life: "I have set before you life and death, blessing and cursing. Therefore choose life, that both thou and thy seed may live." As I faced what I thought was certain death, how desperately I wanted to make that choice! Yet I ultimately decided that even if lying about my religion would allow me to escape, I would not—could not—deny my heritage in this way. This decision, I determined, was also a choice—a choice to live and to die with my identity intact, because of who I was, not who I was not.

In this sense, too, I would continue to be who I always had been, but with a renewed affirmation of what life was or could be and with a more sober and even somber recognition of the terrible surprises that may lie in wait for us all. And just as I had promised, I would use my second life to begin a new part of life: I would bring comfort and joy out of pain, and Peter and I would marry, at last.

The years have passed, the nightmares have ceased, and I do not consciously think of the ending that might have been. But I also have changed in ways that cannot be unchanged. Quiet moments of calm still seem filled with special joy, and I have trained myself, whenever another one of life's surprises strikes, to remind myself that in some sense everything that happens is a bonus. Each time I read of another hostage incident, as such events have come to be known, I relive a moment of terror even as I pray that these hostages, too, may emerge soon from their captivity alive and whole, and that they may also find in their new lives gifts of days that will be cherished all the more because no one has promised them anything.

Robert Jay Lifton has used the metaphor of death and rebirth to describe the experience of survivors of war, death, and disaster. In the aftermath of catastrophe, Lifton has written, whether personal or mass-scale, such survivors can either become mired in a numbing guilt, which Lifton terms psychic stagnation, or struggle forward in a quest for renewed meaning:

> The hard-won "knowledge" of death . . . is precious in the extreme. It takes shape from the struggle to grasp the death encounter and render it significant. Only by coming to such knowledge can the survivor cease to be immobilized

137

by the death imprint, death guilt, and psychic numbing. . . .
What I am suggesting is that to "touch death" and then
rejoin the living can be a source of insight and power.[8]

My ordeal as a hostage lasted thirty-nine hours, but the
internal process of change went on far longer, and these re-
sults linger to this day. I remember how, soon after being
released from captivity, I went to the beauty shop to get my
hair cut. When I told the hairdresser all my news—including
my decision to marry—he responded, in a puzzled tone, "Gee,
rather than get married, I thought you'd want to do something completely different, like have a fling!"
What this man did not understand was that I was already
having a fling—a fling with life. But only then did I also understand why Peter had called his memoir "Living in Doubt."
Living in doubt meant finding the determination, even the
courage, to see doubt through, until, perhaps, it even became
hope. And though nobody could promise me tomorrow, perhaps, if I faced each day and did not turn away, I would also
find the meaning that could make hardship and suffering
worthwhile. That was the challenge, I had found. That was
life. It was time to go forward with this new knowledge—
which was old knowledge—once again.

[8] Robert Jay Lifton, *The Life of the Self: Toward a New Psychology*
(New York: Basic Books, 1976), 115.

5

INVISIBLE LOSSES

THE GRIEFS AND THREATS that Peter and I had faced individually and together had made us feel out of sync and older than our actual age, but we were also weary of sadness and eager to face all the future stages of our still young lives together, both as partners and as parents.

And in this regard we had become in sync again at last. The major challenge of early adulthood, according to Erikson, is to establish intimate partnerships based on mutual cooperation rather than individual competition. Beyond that, the goal becomes "generativity"—creating, "generating," providing for, and caring for the next generation. It is this "concern for establishing and guiding the next generation" that characterizes the mature adult and forms the central, urgent goal of middle adulthood.[1]

Certainly that urge can be fulfilled in many ways, as teacher, mentor, public servant, artist, volunteer. But for

---

[1] Erik H. Erikson, *Identity, Youth and Crisis* (New York: Norton, 1968), 138.

most people it is achieved primarily by "doing what comes naturally"—having children. But what if you cannot be a parent biologically? What if you cannot do what your parents, what marriage, and what life itself have prepared you to do— be fruitful and multiply, as the Bible commands, by conceiving and bearing children yourself?

Stagnation and self-absorption are the dark mirror opposites of care, concern, and generativity. Adults without children, Erikson warned, can become their own children or pets, narrowly concentrating on self-interest and showing little or no regard for whoever and whatever comes next. It is not the lack of children in one's life per se that appears to be the central loss for men or for women. Rather, it is the lack of a vital connection with the next generation.

A recent study by John Snarey of Emory University makes this point more concrete. He found that infertile men who substituted self-centered activities such as bodybuilding or object-centered activities such as home improvement for having children were more likely to divorce and to be dissatisfied with their lives in general than men who instead decided to adopt, become involved with other people's children, or invest in the next generation as mentors, teachers, volunteers, or in some other way.[2]

That is why when people say to me, "Having children changes your life," I respond, "But *not* having children also changes your life." And that is why, in the wake of a pregnancy loss or infertility, the challenge comes in discovering a way to transform the desire to be a biological parent into other positive channels.

The questions posed are many: If we cannot have children, what kind of family, what kind of marriage, will we have instead? Will we form an extended family through adoption? If we don't, is there some other way to transform that urge to be a parent—as teacher, mentor, artist, volunteer? What role

[2] John Snarey, "Men Without Children," *Psychology Today*, March 1988, 61–2.

or roles in the life of the next generation will we play instead? And what if the two of us as a couple cannot agree on what that path should be? Will the end of our dream to be parents lead to the end of our marriage as well?

The questions continue: If we cannot bear a child, what does that say about our manhood, our womanhood, the very nature of our sexuality? Will an invisible, painful yearning for what cannot be leave some part of us emotionally barren and bereft? How do you grieve for the family that may never be? How do you mourn a dream that no one else can see? For the images you spin of yourself as parents and of your children growing through the years are in many ways invisible losses, unseen by everyone but you. They are ghosts that vanish, only to return to haunt.

After two wrenching pregnancy losses and an ensuing struggle with infertility, these were hardly idle questions for Peter and me. Nor are they hypothetical musings for the many couples who find themselves unwillingly out of sync with contemporaries caught up in the new lives of their children and their own new lives as parents. About one in every six pregnancies ends without a live birth—with a spontaneous abortion, a miscarriage, or a stillbirth. Doctors also estimate that about one in six couples has difficulty conceiving as a result of various infertility problems. Often, as with us, pregnancy loss and infertility form part of the same case history.

This is our story, but it is hardly ours alone. Because generativity, in its broadest sense, means caring about what kind of world we leave behind for the next generation and all the generations that come after, the "invisible" losses of infertility and pregnancy loss can carry resonance for us all.

———

First, there was the ectopic pregnancy. The fertilized egg, I learned, had got lost on its way to the womb. It had anchored itself within my left fallopian tube, and there the embryo had grown for close to twelve weeks. By the time my condition

141

was diagnosed, the fetus had long since stretched the narrow walls that confined it; no room remained.

The fetus was trapped, but it lived. At any hour, the doctors told Peter and me, the tube might rupture, and the bleeding that followed could cause shock, even death. The baby for which we had hoped could not possibly live; it would never be born. And if the surgeon did not act immediately to cut it from me, it could quite possibly kill me. Would I please sign the surgical consent form?

I knew the dangers and signed. Shortly before my oldest brother was born, my mother had suffered an ectopic pregnancy. When the tube ruptured, she did indeed go into shock; in fact, she came so close to death that whenever she told the story, her voice took on a distant, hollow ring.

Yet I seized hope from her happy ending: Like her, I would pull through and try once more.

The next November, I conceived again. Confirmation came the day before Christmas—no gift could have been longed for more. Days later, my husband and I celebrated New Year's Eve with friends, who shyly whispered their own happy news: Amy's due date, it turned out, fell exactly one week before mine. The men poured champagne; glasses clinked. Amy and I giggled nervously, then sipped: pregnant ladies, we knew, are not supposed to drink.

For nearly five months, it seemed the perfect pregnancy— no troubles, no traumas. And then, as I sat at my desk on a Monday morning late in March, something warm and wet began to ooze out of me. Four months too soon, the waters had broken. Another hospital consent form. Another lost child.

A double loss. Not only was I miscarrying, with no going back, but this child-to-be was never meant to be at all. I learned several new words: anencephalic; neurotubular disorder; amniotic band syndrome. What did it all mean? The bones in the head had not properly calcified. Whatever part of the brain was left would be grossly damaged. The deformities, I was told, were "incompatible with life."

142

Incompatible with life. Nevertheless, it was necessary that I go through labor and deliver the child. An early, unnatural childbirth. On a Wednesday at 10:30 P.M., after three days in a hospital labor room, I gave birth to a 300-gram stillborn fetus that was incompatible with life.

It would have been a girl. I would have named her for my mother. Already, for months, I had been carrying on inward conversations with little Rachel, my Rachel.

When the nurses placed her before me, she lay still and unmoving in a shiny aluminum bedpan. Clay red, with a tiny head, protuberant eyes, and a cleft lip. The bottom half of a leg was missing. Incompatible with life. She had died before she was born.

Different people have different ideas of how to mourn, and many friends counseled me to deny myself nothing: Go to Saks and buy a new bikini; gorge on imported chocolates; take a trip around the world.

And thinking that some amount of self-indulgence might do me good, I wandered in and out of the various shops in my neighborhood. But even as I grasped a dress fabric, gazed at my reflection in a crystal wineglass, or glanced blankly at the words of a book I had been meaning to read for years, I would realize that nothing I bought, no item acquired, could replace what I had lost.

Nevertheless, one afternoon I yielded. I bought a record of Leonard Bernstein show tunes—so light and airy, how could the music fail to comfort me, cheer me, ease me through an hour? And I did listen with restless pleasure before turning off the stereo, replacing the record in its sleeve, and slipping it onto a shelf. Yes, it had helped me escape for a few moments, but then it had ended, leaving me with the same sense of loss with which I had begun—a barren emptiness.

Volunteer activities yielded more lasting solace, as I became increasingly involved in the work of different charitable, community, and nonprofit organizations. When I went to sleep each night, instead of being plagued by a sense of sadness, I could point to the benefit I helped organize or the writing class I taught to troubled kids as time well spent, but still I would wonder: Would I ultimately be satisfied to make these activities permanent substitutes for children of my own that I might never have?

As I sought an answer, there was more advice to follow. The child could not have lived, friends reminded me. This is simply nature's way. The child was spared. You were spared. Soon you'll try again. What could be simpler than that?

But a lost child and a lost dream are never simple. My fantasy of a perfect, healthy child turned out to be only that —a fantasy. Such lost dreams are made of air; you cannot cradle emptiness. Yet dreams that turn into nightmares must also be mourned: first, the actual fetus, deformed, incompatible with life; and then the perfect child that I had nursed in imagination only. Both the child and the dream had died. Perhaps neither one was meant to be.

Put the past behind you: too often the people who give this counsel have no past to put behind themselves. Then I remembered what a friend had told me years earlier, long before I was ready to understand her advice. She had just miscarried, didn't know if she would conceive again, and so she told me, "Whatever your plan for having children is, don't plan on your plan working out."

But all life is wedded to dreams. With each loss, our dream had grown stronger, less ambivalent. When would reality catch up? We waited, knowing that neither of our lost children —children who were never meant to be—could be replaced or exchanged.

We began to try once more, to visit specialists who might help us—and to force sad smiles when friends assured us that our luck would change. How could they be so sure? I would wonder. I wished I could be as blithely certain as they; but the past had shown me that I could not.

Even as we waited and tried, tried and waited, anger would turn to despair to something like acceptance—and then despair once again. Obsessively I would play and replay every moment of the lost pregnancy and wonder: What had I done wrong? What had I eaten—or not eaten? Had I exercised too much? Not enough? Had I transgressed some unknown moral law in a way so subtle yet so vile that not only I but my unborn child must be punished unto death?

Rationally, I knew that no thing, nobody was to blame—or so the hospital genetics counselor had assured us after the autopsy had been completed. It was a matter of chance—a one-in-a-hundred throw of the dice. Try again, and chances are that this time the dice will go your way.

Perhaps. But the errant throw had come from me, and neither in my dreams nor in my waking life could I escape the nightmare fear that in some way my entire life, filled with loss after loss, had been an errant throw, a miscarriage, dead before birth.

Only now did the impact of the ectopic pregnancy hit me with full force: My mother's example had given me the strength and hope to try again. But after this second loss, at five months and from a different cause, I had nothing left to hold on to except despair.

For in losing this second child, I felt that along with the future, I had lost a most cherished part of my past—the chance to identify with and understand my mother from another perspective as I became a mother myself. I remembered how the dream of becoming a mother had begun long ago, in my own mother's embrace, and even though I could no longer embrace her in this life, I had felt myself coming closer to grasping, at last, the depths of a mother's—my own mother's—care. But now I had lost even the chance to be close to her in memory, and it was as if I had lost her once again.

After the first loss, each new loss reminds you of all that came before. After a pregnancy loss, each new birth reminds you of the child you will never cradle. Most poignant of all, on the day that had been my due date, I received a call from the friend with whom I had sipped champagne so many months before. It was a girl! she announced with joy. Even as I congratulated her, I heard my voice crack.

Still I refused to give in to my pain and determined to be "brave." Only in retrospect do I see that I was determined to overcome the angry envy I refused to confront, as I entered the infants' department at Gimbel's to buy Amy's daughter— her daughter, not mine—the most beautiful present my budget would allow. Only then, surrounded by lace-lined bassinets and row upon row of wide-eyed teddy bears which I longed to present to a child of my own, could I fool myself no longer. As if from afar, I watched myself dash down the escalator, flight by flight, fleeing a ghost that I wished were real.

For several months, every new birth announcement or baby shower remained a trial. Perhaps I had learned too well to observe the niceties of other people's good fortune. Or perhaps I tried too stoically to come to terms with my own bad fortune by studiously avoiding whatever mixed feelings other people's happy news stirred. But the more I denied my ambivalence, the worse I felt.

And there were also instances when I could only be stunned by the insensitivity of supposed well-wishers. One old friend, for instance, advised me that motherhood could be highly overrated, even as she lovingly cuddled her newborn with a smile as beatific as his. On another occasion, just weeks after my second pregnancy loss, I ran into an old school chum, who, sympathetically noting my sadness, asked what was wrong. But when I told her, she responded by launching into a lyrical description of the idyllic existence another mutual friend had with her two kids.

It was only after I found myself abruptly leaving a lunch date with a colleague who could not stop complaining about the little disturbances of motherhood no matter how bluntly I tried to change the subject—"You know how much I wish I were in a position to have those very headaches," I said at one point—that I realized I could no longer stifle my sense of loss with a game smile. I must let my grief play itself out, however long that might take. It was one thing to try to share other people's happiness, I understood then, and another to subject myself to needless hurt.

I tried a different strategy. To close friends I confided my concerns and was rewarded with warmth and understanding. From those whom I knew to be immersed in their new roles as parents, I temporarily withdrew; when we emerged from our different journeys, I hoped, we would be friends once more. With still others, I became adept at expressing interest about their pregnancy or newborn at the start of a conversation, then turning the focus to other aspects of our lives.

Because no matter how many times I tried, a trip to the infants' department still could leave me raw, now when birth announcements arrived—and there were periods when it seemed no day would go by without the mailman bringing two or more—I made sure to choose my presents quickly, or I ordered them by phone. And afterward, I did treat myself to a sweater, a book, an exotic blend of tea.

Baby showers presented a different quandary. I did not wish to appear to abandon my friends, yet I also needed to protect myself. As a compromise, I adopted the seemingly peculiar but understandable policy of arriving early to embrace my friend and dote over the infant—and then quickly leaving. Later, at home once more, I would allow myself to cry.

Some of these strategies may seem obvious, but they came with difficulty, for they forced me to admit that I was hardly the rational, optimistic person I had liked to take myself for. The enemy I battled was within, and nothing I did seemed to quell that sadness. As if I had an illness, it seemed, I must simply wait it out, but also as with an illness, I could take advantage of whatever remedies I could find.

Sometimes, I found, repair work within is acted out in actual renovations. So it was that some months after the second pregnancy loss, Peter and I decided to redecorate our apartment. We would follow most of the blueprints we had joyfully drawn up when we first learned I was pregnant—plans that called for transforming my old study into the baby's room and moving my new study to what had been our dining nook. To carry on with this plan, we felt, was a gesture of hope even if, for the time being, the "baby's room" would be an extra room, a place for future hopes. As I transferred the files, desk chair, and computer from the room where I had discovered I was miscarrying, I felt as if I were saying goodbye to an old grief and an old self. Then I sat down at my new desk and thought about a new book—the book that would eventually become this book.

Such repair work goes slowly, imperceptibly. But then one day, quite without warning, you discover you can smile once more. The branches are budding, a bird whose name you have forgotten begins its song, and you sing, too. You may not yet know it, but the name of that song is hope. After too many months, I began to sing again. I began to hope.

———

But as months and then more months passed, hope was challenged once again.

Our story was not a new story. There was Sarah, who laughed in disbelief when she was told that she, a barren woman, would bear a child. Then there was Hannah, whom the temple priest accused of drunkenness even as she poured out her sorrow—the sadness of a woman who was not able to conceive.

Yet long after hope was past, Sarah bore Isaac, and Hannah brought forth Samuel.

These were the miracles I thought of as I visited my doctor month after month in my quest for a modern miracle—if not by the grace of God, then by courtesy of ovulation tests and fertility drugs, sonograms and surgical procedures.

For a long time, the outcome of my own story remained uncertain. After the ectopic pregnancy and then the second-trimester miscarriage; after renewed hope and still more agonized waiting; after the x-rays, blood tests, examinations, more examinations, "minor" surgery, prescriptions and more prescriptions; after five years of promise and frustration, Peter and I still wandered through uncharted ground in the land of infertility.

The climate is unpredictable there. One day I would wake

up and say, "Get rid of all that medication! Throw away the ovulation chemistry set! Just live your life as a middle-aged married couple and be content!" The next day, I would say, "What do you mean? Look at your nieces and nephew! How can you possibly give up?" The third day, I would say, "Let's think seriously about adoption." And then on the fourth day it would be time to check in with my doctor once again to find out what now?

It was odd how lonely this land could feel, even though there were so many others traveling on a similar course. You see these fellow travelers waiting, patiently, all in a row at the doctor's office, just like you; or gamely pasting smiles across their faces at a mutual friend's baby shower—also just like you.

When certain friends and I would gather, we would exchange not old wives' tales but rather what I came to think of as fertility tales: R. confides that she and her husband have different names for different kinds of lovemaking—there is romance, and then there is baby making. M. presents as tough a front to the world as one can imagine, but, she admits, she cries herself to sleep after each in vitro fertilization attempt fails. S., determined to *do* something, is planning to form a local chapter of Resolve, the national self-help group for infertile couples. By contrast, B. prefers not to talk at all —"Denial works best for me," she says.

Best of all, these friends and I would share the success stories we all longed to hear: The surgery was easier than expected, there should be good news soon. For this one, Clomid worked; for that one, Pergonal; yes, those medicines might work for you, too.

These mutual confidences would bring both comfort (no, you are not alone, and yes, you may have good news yet) and pain (their misery is my misery). You can take courage from someone else's tale, but in the end, your story belongs to you alone. You must decide how to proceed: Does your doctor recommend a more powerful fertility drug or a larger dose of the one you're on now? If that fails, are there other possibilities? Will he hold out to you the last hope—though, given the success rates, it is perhaps the smallest of hopes—of in vitro fertilization?

At the same time, you must measure the odds you're fighting: They are never more than fifty percent for any case of infertility, your doctor may remind you, though probably you do not want to know just how low the percentage can go for more complex cases, like your own.

Certainly, you cannot forget to factor in the risks: What if the surgery leaves your condition no better—and perhaps worse—than before? Thanks for the prescription, Doc, but what are the chances of multiple births? (In some cases, they are as much as one in five.) And could you tell me a bit more about those side effects—rare though they are—that might land me in a hospital bed?

Then, finally, after you have researched the medical options as thoroughly as you can, it is time to look within: How long can you go on, now that month after month of disappointment has turned into year after year of despair?

I heard people advise, "Embrace your infertility. Accept it and go on with your life, whether you decide to adopt or not." On the surface, that always sounded like good advice. But to me the words rang hollow. For that accepting "embrace" entails, first, a giving up of possibility—the tossing off of a dream that one has dreamed for many years. And the death of that dream means finding a way to redefine oneself, to peer into the future and imagine a different self, a different life, a different family—a family of two, and maybe someday one.

What about adoption? Eagerly, I began my research, calling agencies, self-help groups, and adoptive families I knew. But, I quickly learned, with so many couples wanting to adopt, and so few babies to adopt, there may be months, perhaps years, of waiting—with no guarantee of success.

"What, are your genes so precious that you have to pass them on to posterity? Adopt now! A child is a child," a friend chided me when I explained my hesitation, while still struggling to conceive, to open myself to yet another source of potential disappointment.

No, I agreed, my genes were not precious. And whether we ever became parents or not, aren't there still other ways to pass on something worthwhile to younger generations—through teaching or community and volunteer activities, through being an aunt, or just through friendship?

And would life as an old married couple be so terrible a fate? The companionship my husband and I shared was special. Raising children would add many new dimensions, my friends assured me—and they also warned me that it would take others away.

Regardless of the outcome of this journey, I decided, the self that finally emerged would—must—be different from the one that had embarked on it, so many years before. And whether or not my husband and I ever became parents, we knew that something more than dreams would be lost, and perhaps gained.

Having children changes your life, but so does not having them. After too many years wandering in the land of infertility, it was time to pause, step back, gaze into those many possible futures—and go on.

———

But to do that, it was also necessary to look behind and see the past in new perspective, if only to mark the stagnant point from which we knew we must move forward. In doing so, I saw that infertility, like pregnancy loss, is an invisible, intangible loss, a medical condition that is not life-threatening but also not life-giving.

Researchers Patricia Conway and Deborah Valentine have identified nine types of losses that relate to infertility and pregnancy loss, each one discrete and painful in itself:

1. lost fantasies;
2. the loss of genetic continuity;
3. loss of one's self-image as a fertile person;

4. the loss of the successful pregnancy and birth experience;
5. loss of the experience of breastfeeding;
6. loss of the opportunity to move to the next stage in the family life cycle;
7. relationship losses;
8. loss of the parenting experience; and
9. losses for other family members such as potential grandparents[3]

To this comprehensive list, a tenth loss should be added: the potential loss of generativity.

Any single blow may sting, but all these shocks together can leave in their wake a sense of inadequacy ("Why can't I do what comes naturally to everyone else?"), feelings of isolation (particularly from contemporaries raising their families), feelings of guilt ("Am I being punished for something I did?"), misdirected fear or anger ("If I can't get pregnant, my husband will leave me!" or, "It's all *his* fault! Why didn't I marry someone else!"), and a despairing belief that one lacks all control in life ("planned" pregnancies sound like jokes to infertile couples). All these losses must be mourned, along with the unborn children, the lost pregnancies, or the stillborn children whom we long to know and raise but who live only in fantasy.

Precisely because the loss of fertility and the loss of an unborn child are so intangible—there is no body to bury, no actual child to have cuddled and known—mourning can be particularly troublesome.

First, to outsiders—that is, to everyone outside the potential parents—there has been no visible loss. Perhaps no one even knew about the pregnancy while it was viable, much less knew that it ended prematurely. Afterward, there are no standard rituals to mark the event or gather family and friends to mourn together. Similarly, the monthly problems and medical details of infertility are not considered appetizing dinner conversation. Nor is there any set way to commemo-

[3] Patricia Conway and Deborah Valentine, "Reproductive Losses and Grieving," in Deborah Valentine, ed. *Infertility and Adoption: A Guide for Social Work Practice* (New York: Haworth Press, 1988), 44–45.

rate another disappointment each month, except with sadness and despair.

Even when they do seek sympathy and support, these disappointed parents may receive instead a lukewarm response that says that their problems are less important or "real" than other losses and unworthy of a full display of grief. Even well-meant remarks such as "Don't worry, you'll try again soon" or "Nature must take its course" may be intended to comfort, but they often are heard (as I heard them) as belittling comments that do not give full weight to the loss. Another, unintended message may be heard: that the parents are in some way marred, unfit, not "natural": "My whole life is a miscarriage, an abortion, dead before birth," was the internal condemnation I could not escape.

Second, mourning the loss of a fantasy can itself lead to special problems. Freud pointed out, in "Mourning and Melancholia," that deep melancholia—or lingering depression—in the wake of grief derives not so much from the death of a person as from a disappointment or loss of some unconscious object. In the case of pregnancy loss and infertility, that unconscious object is the unborn child and a never-to-be-unfolded saga of family life. All of this has been irrevocably lost, unarticulated except in dreams and through lingering despair and lacerating self-blame—hallmarks both of Freud's melancholiac and of prospective parents experiencing infertility or pregnancy losses.

Lost fantasies are intertwined with lost meanings—in this case, what the lost life of an unborn child means to prospective parents who may never be parents. On the most practical level, factors affecting that meaning could include whether the pregnancy was wanted or planned, whether there was a history of infertility or miscarriage, and how long it took to conceive the child or how many months or years the infertility has persisted.

But on the most profound level, the meaning is inextricably tied with the sense of identity that bearing a child brings with it: Will I be a parent? Will I raise a family? What meaning will my life and my marriage have if I do not? To use Erikson's terms, will I yet find a way to be "generative"—or will I turn stagnant?

For women who have mourned the loss of their mother, part of the fantasy may well include what mine did—the possibility of recapturing a closeness with the lost mother. All these and other individual fantasies and meanings must be articulated, reviewed, and mourned, all at once. And that is why, in the case of a pregnancy loss, a new pregnancy does not necessarily take the place of the lost one, as common wisdom would have it, for the meaning of that new pregnancy will be different.

Perhaps it is no wonder that the effects of such "reproductive casualties," as they are sometimes called, can last for years or go underground, only to resurface later in a different form: crying uncontrollably in the toddlers' department, for instance, or mourning a mother's death all over again; becoming depressed on the occasion of an anniversary or reliving a pregnancy loss after a subsequent loss of another kind; feeling more bitter than sweet when confronted with the news of someone else's child's arrival.

Jack M. Stack, psychiatric director of the Family Health Research Education and Service Institute in Alma, Michigan, a foundation that researches infant and maternal mental health, told me: "I've interviewed people as long as twenty years after the pregnancy loss or miscarriage, and there's still a sense of loss. They become angry, experience sadness, cry. They remember the events of that day just as crystal clear as if it's happening right now. . . . In many of these cases these women had experienced grief reactions but had not completed the grief work. It had affected their marriages and their ability to care for subsequent children."

Although pregnancy loss and infertility are both relatively common, they always come with a shock. We expect things to go smoothly; when they do not, we feel we have lost control of a very important aspect of our lives—our ability to have a family.

Information and education constitute one way to begin to feel in control once more: Genetic counseling after my second pregnancy loss reassured me, at the very least, that nothing I had done was to blame for the loss. Similarly, couples undergoing various infertility tests and procedures also invariably learn the lingo of reproductive technology as they research possibilities and go from one infertility specialist to another.

But however thorough the autopsy on the fetus or however many infertility tests are conducted, a specific diagnosis cannot always be made. Even when a diagnosis is pronounced, the "reason" is often what the genetic counselor told me: "We don't know why it happened; it was just a bad throw of the dice." In all these cases, infertility and miscarriages appear as unexplainable random events that leave the prospective parents feeling vulnerable and angry, knowing that however hard they try to understand what happened and why, and however hard they try again, control remains an illusion.

Moreover, infertility is a chronic affliction, with an endlessly repeated cycle of hope and loss that continues month after month, as conception is attempted and fails once more. Like sufferers of chronic illness, couples experiencing infertility must learn to live with pain and ambiguity and cope with a low-grade sadness that can breed isolation and quiet desperation.

Infertility, like chronic illness, is also not "time-limited," and in spite of each month's disappointment, infertility patients must proceed from treatment to treatment on optimism and faith. Success rates for in vitro fertilization and other new and still experimental procedures remain low, while both the emotional and the financial expenses are high. There is also the embarrassment and the agony of prolonged medical treatments—beginning with various investigative "workups," sperm counts, and x-rays, then moving forward to fertility drugs, surgical procedures, and other regimens, which all told are usually given no more than a fifty percent chance of success, and often less. The procedures themselves, poking and probing as they do into literally our most private parts, can seem degrading and impersonal, adding further stress and anxiety to an already uncertain quest. With so many time-consuming procedures to keep track of—from marking temperature charts to keeping daily doctor's appointments, from setting "appointments" for sex to remembering to mix the right medical "cocktail" of hormones or fertility drugs beforehand—doing what comes naturally never seemed so unnatural.

Yet the longer all these treatments and procedures continue without success, the deeper the couple's emotional rut can become, as they find themselves still running in place, no matter how hard they try to move forward, how many new tests or fertility drugs they try. Having gone so far, they feel, they cannot turn back *now*, and so the months of disappointments turn into years and still more years of dashed hopes.

"When you think about devoting three, five, ten years of your life to infertility, it does affect the quality of your life," Joanne Galst, a psychologist specializing in infertility and pregnancy loss, told me. "It's a very long time to put your life on hold. Women don't buy any clothes because they always hope they're going to get pregnant. You don't make vacation plans because you might need to see the doctor. You set all your money aside because the medical treatments are expensive, and so is adoption. So you don't buy a house or a car. Careers are also put on hold, because you need the medical benefits and you cannot quit, or you can't start a new job when you don't know if you're going to get pregnant. You cannot plan a life outside of infertility, decision making becomes difficult, you become mildly depressed, and that affects your outlook on life, your energy level, your ability to experience joy." In this way, the invisible loss of infertility begins to color and infect the entire visible world around you.

The disappointments of infertility and pregnancy loss also may (and probably will) affect the couple's marriage itself. The reason is this: Men and women don't always have the same fantasies—or the same responses to loss or ways of coping with it—and since each partner may not be able to provide the other's most important form of support, the marriage itself can suffer.

In general, researchers have found that men tend to be more action oriented, seeking distraction—going to the movies or suggesting a vacation—while women dwell on what has happened. In this cycle, the husband's suggestions to go out may be perceived by the wife as unhelpful or uncaring, while the wife's desire to talk about the event may be seen by the husband as obsessive. The two withdraw from each other, and other unresolved strains in the marriage may surface. When their responses don't match, husband and wife may quarrel, nurture bitter silence, or turn away from each other to new interests or love affairs. "I don't want to talk about it!" one partner says, walking away, even as the other shouts, "But who else *can* I talk to!" Instead of forming a new life together, the couple may decide to form new lives separately.

The danger is present even in the "best" marriages. I remember feeling miffed when, after our second pregnancy loss, Peter's initial depression began to subside even as mine lingered on. As we uncorked the champagne to celebrate the beginning of the next year, I could not help but exclaim, "Thank God this awful year is over!" There was a long pause, until Peter said quietly, "But in many ways, this was a good year for me." At that moment, I knew we would have not only to explain to each other but to understand from each other's eyes what this year had been for us, both in joy and in sorrow.

As a result, Peter and I eventually made a pact to set aside time periodically to discuss what was bothering us. "The infertility drugs you're on are making you so tense, it's driving me crazy!" Peter would say. For my part, I called these sessions "going to the dentist," because getting Peter to admit such feelings, I found, could be as difficult as pulling teeth. But, I also felt, it was just as necessary, lest we have another New Year's celebration that left us feeling strangers to each other's reasons to celebrate or be sad.

———

And then what? For some, the treatments and procedures lead to a successful pregnancy and birth. But for many others, the urge to be fruitful remains a fruitless quest that, with so many promising if still untested and often grueling medical options to consider, can continue indefinitely.

Thus, with no external force to say, "Stop, enough!" an internal shift must be made, from focusing on being an infertility patient or a biological parent to being an ex-patient, perhaps an adoptive parent, perhaps a child-free couple, perhaps someone else again. Embedded in this decision is another one—whether you will reach forward to the next generation and "generativity" in some way other than biological parenthood.

When that shift is made, it is said to be a turning point—a moment in which one turns from the past to the future. In *Becoming an Ex*, Helen Rose Fuchs Ebaugh examined the different kinds of turning points that people experience in choosing to leave one identity or "role" in life and take on another, whether it is through divorce, switching jobs, or other means. Although Ebaugh did not examine infertile couples, I believe her findings apply to this loss as well. A turning point, Ebaugh found, arrives in many ways: It can come gradually, over a period of time. Or a single, seemingly insignificant but symbolic action can serve as the straw that broke the camel's back. Time factors, such as the approach of a milestone birthday, also can set a deadline for action. Some people may pose the question as "either/or," as in "Either I get pregnant this month, or we start finding out about adoption." And sometimes an external event—a friend's decision to do something you yearn to do—can give you the courage to change, too.

Similarly, as infertile couples begin to leave this unwanted role behind, they also experience various turning points. For one couple to whom I spoke, the last straw was an unexpected complication during an in vitro fertilization attempt. Was something always fated to go wrong? they wondered. Another couple found their marriage suffering so much that even had they conceived, the damage was done; before proceeding to the in vitro, they decided to file for divorce. Yet another couple, playing one weekend with a friend's adopted child, thought, Why don't we think about this, too? Still others hear the biological clock ticking and wonder, How much longer can this go on?

For Peter and me, the turning point came gradually, as we realized that even if we could not conceive biologically, we must reconceive ourselves—who we wished to be and what our family would be in spite of our various losses. Peter had long since grown weary of our months of waiting—months he now spent waiting for me to come to the same conclusion. Near the end, I would sit alone for what seemed hours, revisiting in memory all the years of our marriage and walking through each one again to determine how we had reached this particular point, *why* we had reached this point without our hoped-for children, and whether there perhaps had been some unseen path that we had missed, to our regret. I would go over each choice in every road again and again, and then again, and always come to the same point—this point, a turning point.

But turn in which direction? I would sit once more, this time to wonder where each new and unknown path would lead. And each of these imagined alternative paths, I realized in retrospect, had to do with what Erikson called generativity —with discovering a way or ways to be connected to the future, whether as adoptive parent, aunt, professional mentor, teacher, or volunteer.

As I considered these choices, I did not yet know what role or combination of roles I would eventually choose. Yet without my realizing it, I already had taken on all the roles I had named but one—that of adoptive parent. Further, by then I had undertaken several article assignments about adoption, ostensibly as a reporter, really to find out for myself how to adopt a child. Even though Peter was not yet as excited as I by the prospect of adoption, I hoped he eventually would be. In any case, my research created the opportunity to speak to adoptive families in a "neutral" forum and help me think through adoption as a real rather than an abstract possibility.

Husbands and wives may cope with and live through loss at a different pace, but eventually they may reach the same point. After a long discussion with Peter one winter evening, I told him I had come at last to the conclusion he had come to several months before—that it was indeed time to give up our infertility treatments and, with them, our hopes of conceiving biologically. "Diane, I've been thinking about something else, too," he responded softly. "Give me those adoption articles of yours to read."

Although that small, undramatic moment could be said to be our "turning point," I see it more as a meeting point, where our different but related journeys through loss converged. But only by talking to each other throughout these same but different journeys and by looking at the many possible futures both independently and together, I feel, were we able to look forward with an ultimately united vision of what our family and what our future would look like after infertility.

Now it was time to embark on the next part of the journey, identifying ourselves as not an infertile couple but an adoptive family-to-be. And as we turned to that new possibility, writing adoption agencies and filling out the necessary forms, we felt that a burden had been lifted and a new life was about to begin.

Yet even in that time of renewal there were any number of tangible objects and routines to give up, discard, and throw away: the ovulation kit, temperature charts, and little vials of medicines, along with the routine calls and visits to the infertility specialist I would not see again.

And what about the maternity dresses I had carefully cleaned and hung in a hidden corner of my closet after my second pregnancy loss, so many months before? I had worn them with hope and put them away with sadness. Eventually, they had become poignant symbols of a hope that was not to be. Now it was time to give these away, too, and hope they would fulfill someone else's dreams.

Then, on a fine April afternoon, as I was preparing for our Passover celebration, I received a phone call from our adoption agency social worker: Would we like to find out more about a little boy born in Pusan, South Korea, that January? We received the pictures and papers just in time to show them to our guests for the traditional Passover seder—a special celebration marking the start of a new season about to be filled with new life and new lives for us all.

———

Our journey had led us through several identities, from hopeful biological parents to infertile couple to adoptive parents—to simply parents. When our little boy, Edward, arrived in our home, aged seven months, and we cradled him in our arms at last, it was as if we had been reborn as a new family—our family.

Our road is hardly the only one, however. For others, the new life chosen is what infertility specialists now call childfree—a phrase that emphasizes choice and going forward, as opposed to remaining childless, without choice. Childfree does not mean a life without children, these experts stress, but rather one in which relationships with children may be formed through means other than being a parent.

Whatever the choice, the greatest danger arises when the path forward is seen as joyless—a second choice that is less likely to lead to renewal than to regret and bitterness. And however far forward a couple moves toward a new life and away from infertility, the fact of infertility will remain a part of their lives, and certain events still may reawaken the memory, if not the actual pain, of infertility and pregnancy loss for both adoptive and childfree couples.

Finally, adoptive families may face reminders, too, as they tell their child how their particular family came to be. In doing so, they will live through the child's loss upon realizing that in order to have gained his adoptive parents he must have first lost his biological parents; and that this family relationship does not have the genetic base claimed by the great majority of the other parents and children within the larger family, community, and school system. One day, I know, Edward will ask, as all children do, "Where do babies come from? Where did *I* come from?" And when that day comes, I know that we must share together the loss that, of all the gifts of love and life that Peter and I would have done anything to give our child, the one gift we were unable to give was that of birth itself.

Perhaps one day I will tell him that in the weeks before his arrival, I began dreaming about discovering new rooms—

rooms that had existed in my house but that I somehow had not known existed until that moment. In fact, I was about to discover a new room—Edward's room: The room that had once been my study and then had remained empty and waiting, waiting to be transformed upon his arrival, even as he himself would transform our lives as a family.

I had another dream—one that replayed a favorite Jewish folk tale my rabbi had been fond of telling when I was growing up, and which I now saw had special meaning:

A rabbi asked, "What can I expect in the afterlife?" So God took him to a damp cave. He showed him a ragged crowd, suffering from hunger and disease. They huddled around a steaming caldron, and the stew inside it smelled good.

"But why are they all groaning?" the rabbi asked. God told him to look closer. Then the rabbi saw that everyone held a spoon, and that the spoons were long and awkward. By the time the people dipped their spoons into the caldron, drew them out, and brought them near, the broth had all spilled out. Besides this, one needed to grip the spoon at the handle's very edge in order to reach the caldron, but the handle was so long that gripping it this way, it was impossible to bring the bowl of the spoon to one's lips. And so everyone was hungry, and this was hell.

Then God led the rabbi to what He said was heaven. It was a similar cave, with the same smell of stew and the same awkward spoons. But here the people were joyous and well fed. They were happy. They were content. And yet it was the same scene.

Now, what made this second place a heaven?

The people had learned to feed each other with their long-handled spoons. They had learned how to cooperate, how to take care of one another, how to nurture one other, and in so doing, they had learned to care for and nurture themselves.

To learn to feed and help and succor each other, in whatever way we can—that is what being a parent means. It is being generative, in the fullest sense.

6

QUESTIONS OF SOLACE, QUESTIONS OF FAITH

Long ago, when I went to sleep each night, I would carefully wrap myself in sheet, blanket, and comforter, and snuggle mummy-like within my sanctuary. My brothers laughed at me, but I had my reasons: If I exposed a single inch, I thought, a witch would fly beneath the blankets to tickle my toes. But if I protected myself, nothing, nobody, could harm me.

Childhood habits haunt us as adults. Each night I still barricade myself, though life has taught me that whether I protect myself or not, nightmares and night horrors will attack me when they will.

It is the nature of life to leave us vulnerable. But I have also learned that being open to life means being open to joy. Since the moment of his arrival, Edward's presence has helped heal old wounds and open new possibilities for happiness—so much so that it is only fitting that his Hebrew name is Isaac, which, literally translated, means "And she laughed." For even as Sarah in the Bible laughed with joy when she was told that in her old age she would be a mother

163

at last, so Edward has been my happiness. And as I listen to my son and my husband sing silly songs together, the music is filled with even more laughter.

And that is why, after having lived through so much pain with Peter, and having arrived at so much joy with Edward, I find it is unbearable to contemplate the nightmare terror of losing either of the loved men in my life. Yet these thoughts are inescapable as I write about the different losses that any of us may encounter.

Not only do I feel great personal trepidation as I begin to explore the potential impact of losses I hope never to encounter. I begin to understand the fear with which others approached me during my times of sadness. For even the most sympathetic condolence caller may find himself thinking, if only in passing, "Thank God, it wasn't my child! Not my husband! Not me at all!" And the mourner receiving sympathy may in turn wonder, "Why did it happen to me!"

Yet in other people's stories we may find journeys that presage the ones we fear in our own lives. And when I approach men and women who have mourned their children's deaths, I find an almost universal willingness to talk and to remember. "This is one way of keeping our children alive," one woman whose son died in his early twenties said to me. After a pause, she added, "And you know, most people don't want to listen."

From bereaved parents, sometimes I hear an edge of anger, even bitterness, but most of all I hear a lingering sadness. "He should have been here to see his sister's wedding," lamented one man whose son died in an accident. "His death left wreckage," said a woman whose son had committed suicide in his early thirties. "I felt very angry with God—and just angry," said another parent, whose daughter had died in her twenties. Angry and despairing, they all spoke of the void that had been left in their lives, for some temporarily and for others perhaps permanently—a void not necessarily of faith but of all meaning to life.

In his study of bereaved parents, sociologist Ronald J.

Knapp identified the existence of what he calls a lingering "shadow grief." It is a chronic sorrow, he writes, that "can be a burden that parents—mothers especially—sometimes must bear for most of their lives. . . . It is characterized as a dull ache in the background of one's feelings that remains fairly constant and that, under certain circumstances and on certain occasions, comes bubbling to the surface, sometimes in the form of tears, sometimes not, but always accompanied by a feeling of sadness and a mild sense of anxiety."[1] It is reminiscent of the shadow Erikson describes as emerging in mid-life and old age if a continuing sense of generativity and hope are submerged by stagnation and despair. But ultimately it shadows the possibility of an inner death as mourners of any age attempt to wrest meaning out of darkness in the wake of every loss.

I saw that shadow when, the summer after I graduated from college, I sublet a rambling house in the Mount Washington section of Baltimore. The owners had asked an older couple across the street to keep an eye on their house, and it was in this capacity that their neighbor Curtis (as I shall call him), a courtly gentleman in his early sixties, with pale cheeks and thick, neatly combed gray hair, stopped by one evening to say hello. Small talk, however, soon turned to more serious matters, as my neighbor told me the story that would never leave him.

Curtis and his wife had had one child, a daughter, he began. She had beautiful blond hair, and she was brilliant. She had gone to a prestigious medical school, had excelled in her studies, and then, on a day like any other, filled for her with the furious rush of a first-year hospital intern's life, something terrible had happened. She had caught a mysterious virus. No one knew how. Two days later, she was dead.

It had happened several years before, he said; his daughter at her death had been only a few years older than I.

[1] Ronald J. Knapp, *Beyond Endurance: When a Child Dies* (New York: Schocken Books. 1986), 40–41.

It was a curious, chilling visit. We were strangers, and when the summer ended, chances were we would never see each other again. Coming and going throughout that summer, I would glance across the street and catch his watchful gaze. Then, catching me catch him, he would wave from his porch or car or wide front picture window, with a forced half-smile.

I didn't think much about these slightly unnerving encounters until the end of the summer, when Curtis took it upon himself to report to my landlord all the details of my life, chronicling dinner guests and imagining parties I never had. When my landlord presented me with these suspicions, I was stunned. With a curious confusion of sorrow, shame, and anger, I remembered how my neighbor had waved and smiled and watched and watched. And now I wondered if he had recorded all these marks against me simply because, whenever I walked by, I had unwittingly cast a shadow across his path—an added shadow that he did not want or need to remind him of all the other shadows with which he already had to contend.

———

The wonder is not that the shadows of grief remain. The greater marvel is that eventually some may begin to lift.

In Knapp's study of bereaved parents, seventy percent of those interviewed had sought comfort in faith; many of them repeated the recurrent hope for meeting again in the afterlife. Linda Edelstein, a psychologist who has researched the long-term effects of the death of a child on mothers, found that a little less than half of the bereaved mothers in her study had consulted a member of the clergy during the first year of mourning.

Even when religious faith per se is not questioned (or there is no faith to question), the moral values and views we hold are challenged. Knapp found that most of the surviving parents in his study had experienced a change of values, particularly in their perspectives on the relative importance of material wealth, status, and worldly goals of success and achievement. However central these values were before the child's death, afterward they came to be replaced by family, community, spiritual, and other concerns, commitments, and responsibilities.

When I read such findings, I think of Job, whose desperate rage could not be tempered by human response alone. It is only in the matching fury of God's voice from the whirlwind, a voice filled with God's anguish at the suffering of the entire universe, that Job's own agonizing questions can begin to be answered.

And when I speak to Shirley*, a woman in her early fifties, it strikes me that she, too, has gone through Job's rage and arrived at a new faith. "Right afterward, I felt very angry with God—and just angry," she begins. "Now, if I had a message to others who went through what I did, it would be, 'Allow God into your life.' "

Her voice is surprisingly soothing, punctuated with sighs and pauses that resound quietly, like musical rests. Talking is hard, but it also helps her, Shirley assures me. Her words remind me of how another mother answered when asked if she or others she knew in her support group would talk to me about their children's accidental deaths: "Oh, people will talk to you; talking helps keep our children alive."

As I wait for Shirley to continue, I recognize the slow, hypnotic cadences of the Pachelbel Canon that she has put on in the background, and pain mixes with tranquillity as the music, the voice, and the story continue to flow onward, like a stream that, at different points along the way, will gush, become calm, nearly dry into a trickle, then twist and swell and become calm once more.

"Where do you start?" she asks, then answers her own question: "It starts with so much pain. With a point where nothing makes sense. Where a twenty-six-year-old daughter dies of leukemia."

The diagnosis had come in May. Then, in spite of chemotherapy, hope, and prayer, Carol died the following March. "Afterward, people said, 'Take it a day at a time,' " Shirley recalls. "But the day was impossible to get through! That summer was very painful. I was listless and restless, and in the fall I could not go back to my work as a music therapist."

During Carol's illness, feeling "angry with God" but seeking answers from him nonetheless, Shirley had consulted a local rabbi and enrolled in a class about the meaning of Judaism. "Through those classes I got in touch with something spiritual that I had never felt before," Shirley says. "I started looking at things in another way. We were all searching in that class.

"I started in that class before Carol's death, and afterward the group was a source of tremendous strength. The spirituality was like a breath of air. Taking a walk in the country and talks with the rabbi and developing that spiritual sense— those were the things that helped.

"Soon, I realized how fortunate I was. I met a woman whose son had died at the age of thirty-two. She was a widow, had planned to remarry, but after her son's death could not go through with it. She did not know how to handle the mourning. And I could see that whenever the subject of her son would come up, she would divert conversation. She would not allow people to talk about this pain. Only then did I understand why people had said to me after Carol's death, Thank you for allowing us to help you through the pain.

"But after the summer, I could not go back to work. The rabbi suggested that I go to a program in clinical pastoral education. I trained to be a chaplain at a hospital, and that was very healing—being with people in intensive care, on the emergency ward, and getting the different perspectives on life.

"I learned from them. I spent time with parents who were losing or had lost children, and they found strength from my example. And I continue to be a chaplain, as a volunteer at a local hospital." She also recently helped organize a Sabbath weekend retreat for parents who had lost a child—an "exhausting" weekend that brought together twenty-five parents, many of whom wrote to her afterward to thank her for her efforts.

"It's hard to make something good come out of this, but doing so helps keep Carol with me," Shirley goes on. "You go through an experience like this, and everything changes," she says, "everything is different. But the thing that seems important to me now is relationships with others and looking inward. I feel I have a ministry, and I never felt that before. I want to be able to do something with what I learned. I know how important it is to be there, to just listen and hold out a hand, without saying a word. . . . I am a great walker, and walking, watching people tend their gardens, I remember thinking one day that this is like Martin Buber's 'I and Thou' —tending something and making it grow. Because what else do we have?

"After Carol died, as I gathered and put away her things, I thought, We spend our lives accumulating things, but what matters is religion and touching people and reaching out. Not in a do-good way but, for me, in a way that is also knowing that Carol is a part of this.

"For instance, right now I am sitting in the bedroom that was hers. After her death, it was hard even to walk by this room, just to look at her empty bed.

"But now I have converted this room into my office. I redecorated and put up a happy flower wallpaper. I feel that out of her death something is growing and blossoming; it's like death and resurrection. It's the way she touched me and touched others. And whenever I am able to help others, it is part of Carol; everything is coming out of her energy, and that is very wonderful."

In this way, Carol continues to play an important part in Shirley's life, even to the point where Shirley tells me, "Carol was the oldest of my three children, and I still think of myself as having three children." Her presence remains with other family members as well: "My youngest daughter was influenced by Carol's taste in music, and recently she recorded a tape she said that 'Carol would have liked' and played it at the grave. It was a very special experience. People are afraid of that kind of experience, but it's important to open yourself to that. An experience like that is not getting stuck; it's allowing yourself to go through the process."

She concludes: "It's hard to talk about this pain because as I listen to myself speak, it sounds corny. But I've also learned to be comfortable with the pain, to feel it and then trust and have faith and forgiveness. It's all related to my concept of God and not putting myself at the center of the universe. God is much more in my center. . . .

"I've walked through the pain," she says. "I've changed, and through the grief process we have to change, reshuffle, and reorganize. I've learned to live more deeply."

Every attachment expresses a particular part of ourselves, but perhaps no relationship in adulthood reveals our inner selves as intimately as marriage. And so as I review my own life cycle of both loss and joy, the very idea of widowhood terrifies me, even though I know that because of Peter's medical history it is a nightmare whose possibility I cannot deny.

I recall how, several years ago, a mystery ailment felled Peter, landing him in the hospital for several days of observation. The doctors assured us that it was not life-threatening, perhaps not even serious, but because no one knew for sure, tests were ordered—tests and more tests.

Living with uncertainty is nothing new for us, but we were worried: What if the cancer had returned, after all? Experience had taught us how to help each other and ourselves, however, and that is why I came to Peter's bedside each day armed with newspapers, magazines, and books.

It's a kind of game we play; our books are our props in our mutual deception. As I attempt to bury myself in the made-up problems of imaginary strangers in some strange land, I know that he knows that inwardly I'm shaking; and he knows that I know what his fears must be. But why should we scare each other more than we are scared already? How better to keep each other's spirits calm than by acting calm? And how better to pretend we're calm than by reading something, anything at all?

Pretend as we might, however, we have entered a different world here. More precisely, Peter, the patient, has been forced to create a world within this world. It consists of that corner of the room containing his bed, nightstand, tray-table, and green plastic guest chair. Because he is hooked up to an IV tube, it is difficult for him to reach, much less dial, his telephone. Above him, the miniature television set supplied by the hospital hangs from a flexible metal arm; inevitably, whenever a nurse or doctor appears, it is shoved far from view, farther from reach. Needless to say, there is no remote control. And when the cord he must pull to call the nurse drops to the floor, he is truly alone. By now he has long since learned the universal lesson of all hospital patients: that the only comfortable position is lying down, and the only activity is waiting to go home.

"A hospital is no place to get well," an old saying goes. And it's true that each patient must fight not only pain and despair but also the tedium that is intensified by rounds of doctors, nurses, orderlies, and hospital trays. How quickly a hospital transforms a person into a patient. First, you don your uniform—the thin blue-and-white cotton gown that stubbornly refuses to snap shut, the hospital robe that you cannot properly slip on because you are hooked up to the IV. Need to go to the bathroom? Here's a bedpan; see you later.

Out of necessity or shyness, we turn away from these little indignities of hospital life. To dwell on them too much is to lose what dignity is left. And so, without naming the new roles in which we have been cast, we simply act: I help Peter bathe, bring him news of the world outside, keep watch over those who keep watch over him. He assures me he is feeling better, reports his doctor's latest report, smiles. Our lives are as bound together here as they are at home; the only difference is that I am not bound to an IV tube.

Amid all the whirl and clutter of this place, there is hardly room for the patient himself, much less a visitor. In the private struggle to retain some sense of order, of dignity, Peter carefully combs his hair, shaves, finds a place for every object: "The comb? It belongs in the top drawer. The magazines go in the one below. Would you hand me my shaver? It's on the shelf behind me, along with the mirror."

A visitor feels a certain sense of trepidation in entering this foreign land, a shock in seeing so familiar a face set against the white glare of the hospital sheets. There is something about these monumental white beds that shrinks even the largest figure, casts a pallor over the ruddiest complexion. Sometimes, as I enter, it's hard not to wonder if I've come to the right room. It's like looking in the mirror after a bad night's sleep; could that really be me? I learn to recover quickly, though. I smile, give a kiss, take out the daily papers and my book, and we begin our charade once more: we are simply reading in a room together; everything will be all right.

Eagerly holding to this final illusion, we turn page after page, even if it is only the pages of *TV Guide*. And for a moment, we try to forget that the pages of our own lives are suspended between chapters—awaiting a test result, a doctor's visit, a specialist's consultation.

We turn the page once more. We chat about a columnist's analysis of Dwight Gooden's recent difficulties, or the peculiar twist of plot in the novel I'm still pretending to care about, and for a moment we succeed in creating a familiar world in this foreign land.

Perhaps it's not the "real world." But our lives are our lives; we live them even as we conjure others in imagination, courtesy of the books upon our laps.

The plot is simple: Peter and I sit reading in his hospital room, dreaming we are in some other room. We wait and wait. Finally, the doctor hurries in. He is smiling, he extends his hand. Yes, he assures us, this novel's happy ending will be our own. The ailment is really no threat; more bed rest and medicine will do the trick; no need to worry, after all.

And then we eagerly turn the page to begin the next chapter, the next book, the next room, to enter in this very real story of our lives.

———

Thus it is that each year when Peter visits his oncologist for his annual exam, the worry is inescapable: What if this time, even after so many years, the x-ray revealed the recurrence of cancer? What if treatment, this time, was impossible? What would I do, widowed and a single mother, alone and yearning for the presence of someone with whom I have spent my entire adult life? How would I continue, and who would I be?

Fearing widowhood myself, I listen to the stories of women who have faced what I fear.

When Harry Green died in 1972, he and his wife, Martha, had been married for twenty-five years—a marriage that Martha, a spryly cheerful woman in her early sixties, describes as "peaceful, passionate, and romantic. . . . I still hear from friends, 'When I was with you, there were times when I almost felt as if I were intruding because you and Harry were so close.' "

But when Harry died, Martha tells me, "I had no idea who I was, and that was a tremendous surprise to me, because I thought I was a very independent and public figure. For twenty-five years, I had been Mrs. Harry Green. And suddenly, she couldn't exist anymore."

They married in 1947. Both were in their mid-twenties. Harry was enrolled at Harvard Law School, and she was Martha Ellis, the executive director of the Massachusetts League of Women Voters. "I remember thinking at the time that I was surprised that this person, 'Martha Ellis,' disappeared and I was suddenly signing letters as Martha Green or Mrs. Harry Green," she recalls.

"Then, suddenly, when Harry died, that person, Mrs. Harry Green, died, too. I hadn't realized how much one takes on the identity of the man in the family, the husband and father."

This second loss—of Mrs. Harry Green—was particularly eerie because throughout her marriage, Martha had played many roles. In addition to being a wife and mother, she had managed local political campaigns, served on the boards of various community groups, worked as director of placement and career counseling for a local college, and, when Harry died, was nearing the end of a graduate program in counseling.

The details of Harry's death are grim. What he thought was a nagging case of flu turned out to be cancer of the pancreas. Within a month of the diagnosis, he was dead.

"We knew that his life was limited, but we didn't know it would be that limited," Martha continues. "They don't know what to do about that disease. He was under such heavy pain medication that last week that he hallucinated, and we sat there, listening to him review a lot of things in his life as he hallucinated.

"Usually, he was discussing business. He was helping a man transfer from one part of the country to another, and he was making suggestions about making the move easier for this man's kids. Well, Ellen, my youngest daughter, was still in high school—the other two kids were in college and came home right away—and I remember her saying that listening to him was helpful because in a sense he wasn't leaving us, he was just going to the office. It sounds odd, but that way of looking at it helped us laugh.

"After Harry died, we had a lot of black humor. He adored these kids, he was crazy about them, and I remember my mother saying the year before this happened, 'What's Harry going to do when all the kids leave home for college? He'll go out of his mind!' And our gallows-humor joke was, Well, he checked out first!

"Hearing these jokes was upsetting for some people," Martha acknowledges. "They thought it was sacrilegious or disrespectful. But we were so raw and seared, it was a release for us. It helped us come together. It helped us speak about the unspeakable.

"It was also quite wonderful that a whole bunch of people came out of the walls to check on me and call me to do things —people I barely knew," Martha recalls. "I couldn't have imagined many of these people even knowing my name, and here they were surrounding me. Maybe they could help me, I think, because I wasn't completely on the floor.

"The other thing that was most helpful was that Harry and I had a very tight relationship. There wasn't any unfinished business. There was no sour piece that we regretted as a couple, and the kids had a very good relationship with him. There was nobody saying, Gee, I wish I hadn't said this or done that. There was no feeling of that at all. There was only a sadness that we couldn't go on together. Our life together was unfinished. But there was no sour piece to regret.

"And I've heard people say, 'Well, George might not like my getting married again,' but I never felt that. Because my marriage felt good, I didn't have any sense that I had to go out and get married again right away. But I also didn't have a sense that I *couldn't* or *wouldn't*."

Still, the pain was wrenching and at times unrelieved. "Harry died in the spring. My youngest daughter went off to college the following fall, and I was entirely alone. My home had suddenly become a place where I just came home and slept. I felt so fragile, I was scared I would go crazy. I thought I would crack up, though I know now I never will because I didn't then. The psychologists wouldn't like it, but I was afraid that if I really got down and processed it the way they say you should, I would never be able to get up again. Nobody would be there to fix me a cup of tea and say, You'll be all right!

"You see, I also had this commonsensical upbringing, which said there is something that has to be done here, and you'd better do it because nobody else is going to do it! And there were a lot of things I had to do! One of which was to take care of myself. The other thing was to make it clear to the children that I was in charge of the family now, not in a bossy way but so they wouldn't have to feel, Well, what are we going to do with our mother? I had to show my kids that I was going to be OK, and they were going to be OK.

"We also had no economic security. I had been in graduate school, and I immediately had to look for a job that would bring enough money. Well, that was something else, having to look for a job when I didn't even know who 'Martha Green' was! But it did force me to come to terms very quickly with what had to be done. The job search gave me a set structure and purpose. Later, when I had found a new job and become director of career counseling at Sarah Lawrence, my job, office, and title provided me with an identity, even when I myself felt a little uncertain.

"But during that time and for a long time afterward," Martha says, "I had a recurrent, eerie sensation: I felt outside of myself, looking in. This feeling lasted off and on for five years. I would go to parties or be presenting on the job, and I found myself off at a distance, looking at this person in the midst of conversations with couples talking about their most recent trip or their remodeled kitchen, or moderating a panel of students at Sarah Lawrence, or out to dinner with some man, listening to his day. It was like watching a play. . . . But eventually I did become comfortable being Martha Green. That's who I am."

———

Fifteen years have passed since Harry Green's death; Martha Green has long since learned who "Martha Green" is; and memories continue to link her and her family to someone whose presence they will always remember and in some way miss. Her story is not that of someone who "gets over" grief but a more realistic one of learning to live with the anguish and loss and change, and of doing so with dignity and love and even humor and hope.

Yet a few days after we spoke, Martha wrote to me, voicing doubts about some of the very strengths she displayed. "Julie and Chuck and their kids came for Christmas," she began. "We had a great time and threw around a few of our usual jokes. I told them you and I had talked, and Julie said: 'How could you manage that? I would have been crying buckets. But then you know what they say about that—we didn't do our mourning right.'

"She also reminded me that several people laid on us the trip about 'The Big C comes from stress.' You've probably gotten that one, too. Every time someone said that to me, it really stopped me. Didn't I take care of Harry well enough? Was it my fault? In rational thought, we knew he had been having the time of his life—beloved, effective, trusted—but that comment was hard to handle."

I was sad to read these words because, indeed, through the years I had been stung by similar remarks. Such words may be meant to help or instruct, but when heard by painfully vulnerable ears, they inflict blame and guilt. There is no "right" way to mourn, only ways that make it easier or more difficult, and for each person those particular ways will differ. The shock of loss in itself leads us to question ourselves unsparingly, to demand reasons of God and the universe. To blame the victim of illness or assume primary blame ourselves is to add one more cruel blow to an already dazed spirit.

The occasional remembrance of sad thoughts and the desire to share a present happiness with someone long gone also are hardly symptoms of pathology. "Remembering an emotional moment, even now—it makes me wet in the eyes," Martha reflected at the end of our talk. "It's not a deep sadness, just an emotion that makes you well up." Then her voice lightened again as she told me about her youngest grandson, Harry Green—a name that clearly carried not the sadness of loss but the resonance of care and a generation-spanning legacy of family love.

———

As I think about the many different ways of living through each kind of loss, I recall one final conversation. "Why, those pearls are so lovely, so—delicate!" The young blond woman in white smiles sedately as she points to the rose-white strand of baby pearls, each one smaller than the smallest early-June pea, that I happen to be wearing that day. She is a hospital nurse who works with chronically ill children and adolescents. Some of them have had a better time of it than others, she tells me; almost all of them are living in doubt as to what the future holds in store for them. Her expression—faintly expectant, with a hint of wrinkled sadness about her large blue eyes—says she is used to hearing about other people's problems, and she is visibly glad to find someone interested in listening to her, for a change.

She also seems glad to have found a subject other than grief and illness. "You're right to wear them," she tells me, pointing to the pearls again. "In fact, pearls *must* be worn. There's something about their surface. They interact with the air, with the fabric of your dress, with the oils of your skin. That's why every strand of pearls is different, unique. They *become* different, over time. After a while, they take on your own special patina, no one else's.

"And you know"—she pauses, thoughtfully, before continuing, her mind returning to other concerns already—"the way people cope with things here in the clinic—it's the same. Each person develops his own slightly different way of coping with what he's going through. It's as if they've each developed their own special patina, like a patina of pearls."

That night, I held the small, rose-white pearls against the pale yellow light from my reading lamp. Each tiny jewel gave off a pale and hazy luster. I wondered, was this mixture of shade, sheen, and color unique to me? If so, I thought, this special patina—of pearls and of the soul—is merely an outward sign of what goes on within. So that as the journey continued and life continued, the colors would continue to change—through all the different shades and hues of the different stops along the way.

I think it has to be that way for every mourner, whomever he or she has lost. Otherwise we would wear the patina of blackness, and only blackness, forever.

7

A
TANGIBLE ABSENCE

ONE MORNING shortly after my mother died, a hesitant tap on the shoulder stopped me as I left the synagogue where I had just finished saying the mourner's *Kaddish*. I turned to face a fellow morning-service "regular"—a tall, gray-haired gentleman with a football player's thick build. "I don't mean to be presumptuous," he said in a soft voice. "I know you're very sad right now. But I wanted to tell you that I went through all that, too, when my father died several years ago. And here's the thing: Believe it or not, I am as close to my father now as when he was alive! Maybe even closer, because I have come to understand him better. He is inside me, I hear his voice. We are still that close." Then he smiled and waved goodbye, leaving me to ponder words that I began to understand only years later.

What he meant, I think, was that our dead inhabit us like ghosts. The trick, as he knew then and I have learned since, is to befriend them rather than have them haunt us. They will greet us on sad anniversaries as well as in joy. We will imagine a deceased parent's response to her grandchild's arrival;

or we will call back from memory the words or actions of the one person to whom we would have turned were he or she still there. And eventually, when we hear that voice again, it will bring not just pain but comfort and resolution.

The words we speak and hear in that inner conversation become our links to the past. They also are our gateway to a future that our dead will never know but in which we ourselves must live. "Only connect," E. M. Forster wrote—a motto that applies to the dead as well as the living, for how are we to discover our future if we do not come to terms with our past?

At first, however, the threads that connect past to future appear frayed and fragile, perhaps broken altogether. The fabric of life itself seems rough and ugly, without pattern. The struggle to reweave the strands, one by one, can be tedious and delicate, and every one of us will go about the task in a different way. For some, the pain is so overwhelming that the biggest challenge will be to discover a reason to repair at all. At the same time, each loss will leave its particular imprint, depending on the centrality of the relationship, the age of the deceased, and the circumstances of *your* life at the time of his death, the presence or absence of emotional conflicts and other unfinished business, and the way in which the loss occurred.

Yet gradually a different figure can emerge from the tapestry even if, at certain seasons and in certain types of light, the scars of damage can still be seen. And when seen in perspective, that changed figure may be perceived as carrying meaning and purpose, after all. Then you look some more, and you see that the figure is you.

———

The content of that new meaning and the renewed sense of identity to which it gives birth will differ for each person, whether it means changing an inner perspective or outward style of life, becoming a wounded healer, discovering religious faith, turning activist to found an organization, or finding some other path.

For me, that new meaning revealed itself to me as I became more and more bonded to the future—to my son, Edward.

Peter and I had spent the final weeks waiting for our little boy's arrival as most new parents do, waking each morning wondering if this will be the day of days. But the herald for our new arrival would be not labor pains at midnight but an early-morning telephone call from our adoption agency. Instead of a hospital birthing room, our delivery room was to be the Northwest Airlines terminal at New York's Kennedy Airport; and the new member of our family would be not a squalling newborn but a sophisticated seven-month-old international traveler from South Korea, whose first photographs we had framed months before.

Even as we filled out the extensive application forms and questionnaires, then proceeded with the series of meetings and interviews (called the home study) required by our adoption agency, we had shifted our focus from the idyllic dream of bearing a child to the concrete details of what it means to rear a child. This may sound simple, but when you see only roadblocks before you in your quest to have a child, your vision can stop with the first imagined moments of joy as you hold your longed-for child in your arms at last. Daydreams and fantasies may end here, but in real life—the expanded family life we had dreamed of—it is only the beginning of a new chapter, the start of a new life for all.

We had thought through our deepest reasons for becoming parents, and in doing so we had developed far broader definitions for mother and father than the ones furnished by biology. For passing on a genetic heritage is only one small part of the much larger and more important continuing role that parents play—a role we had come to see as passing on love and caring and whatever lessons of life and wisdom we could to the next generation, just as our parents had given these and so many other intangible gifts of spirit to us. Knowing this, we also knew that when you finally do cradle your child, what matters is not the color of his eyes or skin or hair, but the wondering gaze that greets you and the love that your smile conveys.

Then, on an April afternoon nine months after we first approached our adoption agency, we received news that its affiliate agency in Seoul, South Korea, was taking care of a little baby boy who had been born five weeks prematurely on January 19. "He's healthy, and his picture's really cute," our agency social worker purred over the telephone. Were we interested in hearing more? The photographs and other paperwork arrived by express mail the next day. Until then the word "bonding" had always had an abstract sound for me, but the moment I saw his dark eyes and determined stare, I knew what bonding meant.

Psychologically, we were already parents, dreaming about our baby boy. But, our agency warned us, we would still have to wait up to four agonizing months more for all the necessary paperwork to be completed. During that joyful yet anxious time ("His picture seems so close; why can't he come here right *now!*" I inwardly demanded), the agency wisely arranged a meeting of other waiting couples. On an early summer evening, we and four other "expectant" couples gathered together, introduced ourselves, and proudly showed off our babies' photographs. "Wasn't it obvious that our baby was the cutest!" I heard myself declare to my husband afterward. Already, the gushing had begun.

At last we received confirmation that our little boy would arrive in New York on August 25. We could hardly contain our joy, but our agency prepared us not to expect laughter, at first, but rather the sadness of an infant uprooted from the familiar sights, sounds, smells, and tastes of his foster home and unable to express this confusion and loss except through crying, tears, and, quite possibly, a temporary withdrawal from or even rejection of his new parents. He could be very subdued or very active, we were warned; eat very little or consume far too much; refuse to sleep, or sleep for endless hours.

Thus prepared for a squalling, squirming bundle, we were

greeted instead by a wide-eyed little gentleman whose subdued but watchful gaze seemed to soak in every new detail
with quiet intensity. But if he was busy scrutinizing Peter and
me, we were as dreamily enraptured as only new parents can
be. Even as he was placed in my arms, I felt surge through
me an urgent sensation of love, infatuation, and responsibility.

From the jubilant mood of the airport, we proceeded to our
home and, once there, to the first practical challenges of parenthood: not only diapering, bathing, and feeding Edward
but, more than that, helping him get used to his new family
and get over the grueling jet lag left by his eighteen-hour
flight. Those first few days and nights were both exhilarating
and tiring, filled not only with our mutual discovery of one
another, and the warmth of a household filled with new life,
but also with the nagging crankiness of Edward's jet lag and
periodic spells during which he would cry disconsolately for
his "um-ma," his Korean foster mother.

To make things easier, we tried to make the unfamiliar as
familiar as possible. In Korea, our agency told us, it was traditional for all family members to sleep on mats on the floor.
To make Edward's crib seem less foreign, therefore, I placed
the mattress as low as possible. I also decided against
bumpers, so that he could see all around him, unimpeded.
Even so, when Edward woke in the middle of that first night
and I tried to comfort him by going to sleep on a quilt on the
floor beside his crib, his tears grew wilder than before, as if I
had only reminded him that I was not the person he wished to
see there. But, comforted and cajoled at last with loving hugs
and lullabies, he awoke the next day with an eager if somewhat anxious look and began playing on that same quilt on the
floor as if it were the most natural thing in the world.

Our agency also alerted us not to expect Edward to have
reached all the developmental milestones listed in the various
child-care books: First, Edward had been born premature;
second, in Korea babies tend to be held and cuddled more,
whereas in America we tend to stimulate them more. In fact,

although Edward had just turned seven months, he was not yet sitting up or turning over. But, I feel certain, the secure hugs he had received in his foster home also helped him feel comfortable in the arms of his new parents.

Alert to his own possibilities, Edward quickly attacked an infant's play gym a visiting friend had brought us, thrust his arms forward with intense delight when I placed him on my lap in front of the piano, and began exploring his new environment with the relish of discovery. Within days he seemed to leap ahead weeks—beginning to turn over, sit, babble, and giggle, even as glimmers of what we now know to be his naturally bright-eyed look of cheer broke through with increasing frequency. For this reason, we were at first puzzled when he seemed uninterested as we would stroll down a quiet street to our local playground and park. Only when we took a different route, walking directly into the bustle of city life, did he lift up his eyes and turn his head to stare at every sound and face. Was it the activity alone that attracted him, I wondered, or did that street in New York remind him of the area in Seoul where his foster family lived?

Perhaps we'll never know that answer, but in these and other ways we tried from the start to establish for Edward a secure base of love and affection. For however a child comes into your life, he is your child. We had waited a long time for Edward, and now he was home. It was not only a happy ending, but a beginning for us all.

————

With Edward's arrival we had grown from a family duet to a trio. At the same time, as I looked into the mirror I saw someone whose sadness had turned into a smile that proclaimed, "I can't believe how happy I am!" In my voice, too, I heard a new tone. It murmured softly in response to Edward's cries and giggled as delightedly as he.

Often Peter, Edward, and I would sit at the piano, Edward on my lap. As we sang and talked and laughed—all three of us together trying to make sense of the nonsense of Edward's babble—it would sometimes strike me that I could hear in the background of this joyful music echoes of themes that had been transposed from one key to another, from melancholy resignation to harmonies made all the sweeter by the long struggle to find them.

Now Edward and I would look at the old family photo album, and I would see familiar faces as if for the first time, through Edward's eyes: "Look! Here's Grandma Roselda, Mommy's mommy! If she knew you, she'd give you a big kiss and say, What a wonderful grandson you are!" I would shout these words gleefully while Edward squealed with delight, even as I kissed and hugged and held him in his grandmother's stead.

It is a happy game, but it had grown out of sadness. How else except through imagining my mother's joy at Edward's arrival, I had wondered, could I bear my sorrow at her absence? Who could have predicted that this game would become so enjoyable both for Edward and for me that a glance at my mother's picture now elicits one of Edward's brightest grins?

At the same time, the inward conversations that I had carried on with my mother in times of confusion and sorrow now bubbled forth in the form of nurturing memories of my own growing up. These remembrances brought multiple insights, teaching me to be a better mother to my son as I recalled the care with which my mother had mothered my brothers and me. And although I could not converse with her in person, these dialogues brought us closer in ways I could not have imagined, echoing the words my unknown comforter had given me at the synagogue years before. For now I found myself viewing her not only from a daughter's perspective but also from the perspective of a mother; understanding her care not only as the receiver of love but also as a giver, wishing to learn from her example, in memory, how she had managed to make so many difficult moments seem simple.

In these and other ways, as Edward grew, so Peter and I grew, learning that joy feeds upon joy, even as sadness had fed upon sadness. "I've never seen you look so happy!" I would say to Peter, and he to me. That growth also has yielded the creation of a new entity altogether—a family with its own special traditions: the celebration of "Family Day" each year on the anniversary of Edward's arrival; teaching Edward to say "Shalom" in recognition of his Jewish heritage, and at the same time decorating his room with a wall hanging and other mementoes from Korea. And as we go through the photograph albums that tell the story of Edward's arrival and the formation of our family, I hope that someday Edward, too, will come to tell this story in his own way, from his own perspective—the story of how, out of so many different losses in his life and in ours, there came the possibility for so much enduring love and family happiness.

And so the past remains alive in the present, resonant with themes that have undergone so many transformations from minor key to major that we hear a different music altogether, family harmonies carrying us all into the future together.

Even as Peter, Edward, and I were defining ourselves as a family, healing also came for me through the more solitary acts of writing and remembering. "How could you bear to write about so much sadness!" friends would ask when I mentioned this book. But writing can be not merely a means of expressing grief; by making sense of loss, it can stay grief's ghosts.

Peter and I had learned these lessons through personal experience. So it was with particular interest that I read the observations of British psychoanalyst Anthony Storr: "The [artistic] process is an effort to come to terms with loss in which pain is accepted, rather than an attempt to deny loss or to escape from it," Storr wrote.[1] Rather than confiding his sadness to a friend or counselor, the artist turns to art, finding both solace and new meaning in the work itself.

[1] Anthony Storr, *Solitude: A Return to the Self* (New York: The Free Press, 1988), 127–8.

This search for meaning in the wake of loss is nowhere better expressed than in the works of two of my personal literary heroes—writers who at first seem very different but whose personal histories make them brothers not only in art but in loss: the sixteenth-century French philosopher-essayist Michel de Montaigne and Victorian England's most celebrated poet, Alfred Lord Tennyson.

Both writers' best-known and most widely acclaimed works —Montaigne's *Essays* and Tennyson's *In Memoriam*—were spurred by the untimely death of an irreplaceable friend, tragedies that became both personal and artistic turning points. Montaigne was thirty when his friend and colleague Étienne de La Boétie died. Tennyson was twenty-three when his college companion, fellow poet, and brother-in-law-to-be, Arthur Henry Hallam, died suddenly from a stroke.

Both friendships were platonic, yet both contained a powerful intellectual and emotional intensity. For both Montaigne and Tennyson, these losses set off chain reactions of personal depression and religious doubt that gave rise to the profound philosophical and artistic ripening that imbues their subsequent works.

In this sense, their personal losses can be said to have become every reader's gain. From a psychological point of view, their stories also reveal the healing powers of art in helping to repair the wound and mend the damage within. Finally, both the *Essays* and *In Memoriam* chronicle their authors' search for a renewed meaning to life and a new understanding of religious faith in a world shattered by personal loss.

Thus it was that, caring deeply about these same concerns and already embarked on my own search, I began yet another quest, reading everything I could about Montaigne and Tennyson.

Born into the nobility of southern France in 1533, Montaigne spent his first thirty years discovering who he was. He went to school, traveled, enjoyed society, flirted without marrying, and in his private studies cultivated the love of learning and the skeptical view of human nature that characterize all his writings. He was diligent in his duties as a member of Parliament, but he seems to have followed his father's profession of lawman and statesman more out of family duty than from personal commitment. In this regard, it might be said that he was drifting—a man who possessed learning, charm, and the privileges of his noble estate but seemingly little inner purpose or direction.

Then, in 1559, Montaigne met La Boétie, a scholarly colleague in Parliament who was two years older than he. Whereas Montaigne dabbled, La Boétie showed seriousness and commitment in his various roles as husband, distinguished public servant, and noted thinker and author. Despite these outward differences, however, the two men quickly became devoted friends, more deeply attached than brothers, constantly engaging in passionate intellectual discourse.

On August 9, 1564, La Boétie fell ill and sent for his friend. Montaigne spent most of the next nine days tending La Boétie and comforting his family, until the end.

Not only did the courage and humanity with which the stoical La Boétie faced his end greatly affect Montaigne's personal philosophy. His friend's sudden death affected the very course of the life left to Montaigne.

For the next two years, Montaigne's biographer Donald Frame tells us,[2] Montaigne sought refuge from his grief in various love affairs, searching for consolation, if not an actual replacement for his friend. But when Montaigne did marry, his wife's intellectual and emotional companionship suffered

[2] The biographical information in this chapter comes from three books by the noted Montaigne scholar Donald M. Frame: *Montaigne: A Biography* (San Francisco: North Point Press, 1984); *Montaigne's Essais: A Study* (Englewood Cliffs, N.J.: Prentice-Hall, 1969); *Montaigne's Discovery of Man: The Humanization of a Humanist* (New York: Columbia University Press, 1955).

The quotes from the *Essays* are taken from Donald Frame's translation, *The Complete Essays of Montaigne* (Stanford, Cal.: Stanford University Press, 1965). Another source on the life and work of Montaigne was *The Autobiography of Michel de Montaigne*, Marvin Lowenthal, ed. (Boston: Houghton Mifflin, 1935).

by comparison with the rapport he had established with La Boétie. (Throughout the essays, Montaigne scoffs at the notion of friendship between husband and wife as an impossibility and, in any case, no more than an inferior substitute for the truer spiritual friendship between men.)

Without his friend, Montaigne nonetheless continued his duties in Parliament for several more years. When circumstances forced him to leave in 1570, however, he threw himself into the publication and preservation of La Boétie's poetry and political discourses, as if to find in his friend's work the companionship he missed. Then, still suffering from a lingering sadness at the loss of his friend, Montaigne retired to the privacy of his study and began the desultory writing project that eventually became the *Essays*, a document that in many ways served as yet another method of searching for, inwardly discoursing with, and partially recovering his lost friend.

Frame notes that Montaigne himself admitted that if it had not been for La Boétie's presence in his life—and then his sudden, tragic absence—he probably would not have set about writing his essays at all. "I needed what I once had, a certain relationship to lead me on, sustain me, and raise me up," Montaigne commented in explanation of why he turned to the writing of essays.[3] If La Boétie had lived, this passage suggests, Montaigne would have possessed no reason to make his thoughts public but would have addressed private letters to his friend instead.

But with no one to whom to reveal his most personal thoughts either in person or through letters, Montaigne was forced to find a different method of discourse and form of expression through which to rework his view of life—and now of death.

The essays allowed him to search for and recover, if not La Boétie himself, then his equivalent—a kindred spirit in imagination. By revealing his thoughts in public, Montaigne wrote,

[3] *Montaigne: A Biography*, 83.

he hoped he might search out and reach another soul with whom to share the special fellowship he had lost: "Besides this profit that I derive from writing about myself, I hope for this other advantage, that if my humors happen to please and suit some worthy man before I die, he will try to meet me."[4] In these and other ways, the essays became Montaigne's partial substitute and consolation for the loss of his beloved friend.

The subject matter of the essays bespeaks the continuing influence of Montaigne's grief and loss, but also the healing consolation provided by his writing project. The essays are filled with references to ideal friendship—references that often invoke the memory of La Boétie:

> As I know by too certain experience, there is no consolation so sweet in the loss of our friends as that which comes to us from the knowledge of not having forgotten to tell them anything and of having had perfect and entire communication with them. O my friend! Am I better off for having had the taste of it, or am I worse off? Certainly I am better off. My regret for him consoles and honors me. Is it not a pious and pleasant duty of my life to be forever performing his obsequies? Is there an enjoyment that is worth this privation?

Throughout the essays, and especially in the early ones, Montaigne seems preoccupied with mortality, the fleeting quality of life, and the consequent vanity, even absurdity, of so many human wishes. He reflects again and again on the meaning of life within the context of the inevitability of death —a wrestling with meaning and faith that suggests the inner turmoil set off by his friend's untimely death.

For Montaigne, writing served as a way of reflecting upon questions of meaning and faith that could never have been entirely resolved, even if La Boétie had lived to discuss them with him. But Montaigne did not have the option of raising these questions with La Boétie; moreover, if La Boétie had

[4] Ibid., 82.

lived, these questions might not have troubled him much to begin with.

Thus, when Montaigne writes, "to philosophize is to learn to die," or "to learn to die is to unlearn servitude," he no doubt had the example of his friend's courageous death in mind. For if his friend's sudden, stoical leave-taking had demonstrated one thing, it seems to have been that the more equitably one comes to terms with the prospect of death while still among the living, the freer, less fearful, and more richly textured life itself can be.

This stoical humanism, Donald Frame notes, was far more characteristic of La Boétie than of the more free-spirited Montaigne: "We may argue with a living friend and still idolize his values when he dies." In death, however, the dialogue must be internalized, the deceased's responses only imagined. Montaigne went even further, idealizing and internalizing his friend and modeling his own philosophy on his friend's. The Montaigne of the early essays, Frame writes, is far closer to the measured, Socratic La Boétie than to the high-spirited youthful Montaigne.

Eventually, Montaigne cast off this mantle, discovering a more flexible philosophy of his own. But he still felt what amounted to physical pain when he remembered his friend's death, and he acknowledged his friend's pivotal influence until the end of his life.

Tennyson met Arthur Henry Hallam while they were both students at Cambridge, where they shared a mutual enthusiasm for poetry. Like that of Montaigne and La Boétie, their friendship provided them with an intellectual and emotional intimacy they had discovered nowhere else. When Hallam became engaged to Tennyson's sister Emily, it seemed that Hallam and Tennyson truly would be brothers.

But in the fall of 1833, while accompanying his father on a trip abroad, the twenty-two-year-old Hallam fell ill and suddenly died of a stroke caused by an apparently congenital malformation of which no one had been aware. The shock to the Tennyson family was terrible; Emily and Alfred had lost both a friend and a prospective husband and brother. Yet each Tennyson grieved differently. Emily at first was more visibly shaken than the seemingly calm Alfred, who brooded on his loss in solitude. As time went on, however, Emily was able to rejoin society more quickly than her brother, and in 1841 she married Richard Jesse, a navy lieutenant whom, ironically, she had met while visiting the Hallams shortly after Arthur's death.

Tennyson, by contrast, remained inwardly shattered by his loss, moving through life like a rudderless ship. "He kept up the motions of normal daily life, but he had lost his most important anchor to reality," Tennyson's biographer Robert Bernard Martin wrote of the poet's response to Hallam's death. "His one remaining resort was to poetry, used as a narcotic for an existence made temporarily meaningless."[5] Indeed, within days of receiving news of Hallam's death, Tennyson began composing the first of a long series of elegiac stanzas, which would be published seventeen years later as *In Memoriam:*

> *But, for the unquiet heart and brain*
> *A use in measured language lies;*
> *The sad mechanic exercise,*
> *Like dull narcotics, numbing pain.*

> *In words, like weeds, I'll wrap me o'er,*
> *Like coarsest clothes against the cold:*
> *But that large grief which these enfold*
> *Is given in outline and no more.*

Sir Charles Tennyson, the poet's grandson, reflected on the effect Hallam's death had on Tennyson's entire world view: "These months of suffering intensifed the desire, which was

---

[5] Robert Bernard Martin, *Tennyson: The Unquiet Heart* (New York: Oxford University Press, 1980), 184.

to haunt the poet throughout his life, to find an answer to the great and insoluble questions, regarding the survival of the human spirit, the freedom of the human will, and the existence of a divine purpose guiding the universe. Now, under the first shock of his great grief man's fleeting existence seemed to have lost all meaning for him."[6]

The shock of personal loss naturally forces us to question whether there is any meaning or order in the world. Religious faith bolsters many people. But the times intensified Tennyson's rootlessness and despair. Recent geological and scientific findings concerning the evolution and extinction of species were calling faith itself into question throughout the Victorian world. Still feeling his loss, Tennyson turned his attention to finding a way to reconcile faith and science—a quest that became inextricably intertwined, in Tennyson's mind, with rediscovering a reason and order to life in the wake of Hallam's sudden, apparently pointless death. It is no wonder, then, that *In Memoriam* is at once a chronicle of grief and a search for meaning in a world whose brightest possibilities for happiness and human comfort have been not only shattered by personal loss but cast in doubt by religious skepticism.

Tennyson originally wrote the many verses of his poem not for publication but as a purely personal reflection, to chart his course of grief and doubt. When he finally did publish his work, in 1850, Tennyson regarded it, he wrote, as "a kind of *Divina Commedia*, ending with happiness." That is, like Dante's work, *In Memoriam* is a spiritual journey that leads through the hell of despair to the recovery of faith.

Tennyson's work reveals all the melancholy moods of grief, doubt, loneliness, and despondency over the course of a three-year span. Each lyric is a separate thought that is also linked to what came before and will come later, as initial despair gives way to a final renewal and affirmation of human joy. The

[6] Sir Charles Tennyson, "In Memoriam," excerpted in the Norton Critical Edition of *In Memoriam*, ed. by Robert H. Ross (New York: Norton, 1973), 105.

poem begins with Hallam's death and the return of his lifeless body from Vienna for burial, and it ends with a marriage song in celebration of Tennyson's sister Cecilia and her groom-to-be, Edmund Lushington. In between, Hallam's life, friendship, and truncated promise are reviewed in detail. Regret and gloom are given full vent, as are the poet's painful longing, even pining, for lost companionship. Castigating himself as worthless when compared with Hallam, the poet evinces a survivor's guilt—why did he die rather than I? Perhaps, the poet reflects, there may be a chance for us to meet again in another world, where life and its petty concerns are not as fleeting as in this one. But faith also is in doubt: can faith survive in a world of science?

The poet argues back and forth, but ultimately he asserts that we must and can recover faith. This belief in turn begins to ease the pain of personal loss. Slowly the recognition develops that Hallam's influence, and thus his love and spiritual presence, will continue to be felt despite death. The poet can look forward to the possibility of renewed happiness and renewed faith, at last.

Tennyson grappled with these questions in the solitude of his study, his poetry mirroring his progression from unconsolable grief to a new accommodation with the world. It is probably no coincidence that in the same year that he published *In Memoriam* Tennyson finally married, as if to declare the end of one chapter and the beginning of another not only in his poetry but in his personal life. In this way art did not merely provide Tennyson with solace and escape, it afforded a means to work through pain and doubt, to discover meaning in the wreckage left by his friend's death, and ultimately to build a new vision of life's possibilities.

For Tennyson and for Montaigne, writing served as a means of expressing grief and a way of living with it, and they are hardly the only artists whose lives and visions were indelibly shaped by personal loss. I think of Charlotte and Emily Brontë, whose early lives were punctuated by the deaths of their mother and older sisters, one relentlessly following the other. After his mother's death, Johannes Brahms composed the haunting trio for horn, piano, and violin as a memorial; it is a work that also comforted me after my mother's death.

Clearly, not everyone who tries to express his experience of loss in words, music, or images will turn out to be a Montaigne, Tennyson, Brontë, or Brahms; such genius is rare.

But the struggle of a great artist to repair what has been rent can help all of us. It is art's solace and one of its great gifts. As we listen to the artist's voice, we hear our own. In the same way that Tennyson and Montaigne had served as my philosophical guides and Brahms as my musical release, the artist's struggle to transcend his pain can become the seed for many others' hope, transforming a personal journey into a vision for us all.

For me, as I write these words, I see that vision has become one of knowledge tinged with pain but also with hope. Instead of feeling lost, I have learned to take joy in what I have found.

In addition, I see that my journey through grief has oddly mirrored an actual journey I took several years ago while traveling through France with my husband and in-laws, when we went to see the prehistoric paintings in the cave at Rouffignac, near Lascaux, in the Dordogne Valley of France.

As you approach it, the arched mouth to the cave is mossy and inviting. Step inside, though, and a shadow falls, and the farther you go, the darker, more mysterious, and more frightening it becomes. Nor can the summer's blistering warmth penetrate these thick gray walls of rock. You want to put on a sweater—quick—before you catch cold.

Still shivering, and before your eyes have adjusted to the dimness, you board a small, toylike electric train that will take you deeper and deeper, through several miles of underground caves. Even before you begin, though, the sudden cold, the darkness, the low ceilings and narrow walls, all have contributed to a sense of exquisite claustrophobia: Should you wander from the group, you would indeed be lost in a maze, forever and alone.

The tour guide speaks in rapid French, but as in a dream,

your high school fluency returns, and you begin to understand his words. Here, in approximately 11,000 B.C., primitive hunters painted the most difficult reaches of these walls and ceilings with the outlines of mammoths, bison, horses, and other beasts. Look! There they are all around you, ready to charge!

Deeper and deeper you go into the cave, through cold and darkness, along an endless maze of twists and turns that feels like the dreaded journey of death itself. At last, the train stops. You are instructed to look up—not toward heaven but to the black ceiling above you. Suddenly, the guide's flashlight beams so brightly that it momentarily dazes. And there, at the very heart of the cave and at a seemingly unattainable point, high above a hidden abyss, you gradually perceive a faded, barely discernible, oddly misshapen form above you and realize that it is the one human figure in this entire cave.

How puny and insignificant I felt at that moment! I had entered that cave feeling that I was caught in a maze, unable to find my way out from sadness, and that my own personal Minotaur, my grief, would surely find and slay me, no matter how clever my escape. I would fail at my attempt to play Theseus and rescue myself; nor could I see Ariadne's thread, leading the way out.

Yet as I stood in the cave and looked above me, I saw something more. For wasn't that single human figure also a precursor of Theseus, the hero, who would travel into the heart of the darkest unknown labyrinth, slay the terrible beast that threatened him, and return into the light to live his life once more?

Luckily for us, an army of Ariadnes, in the form of engineers and paleontologists, had left an easy trail for us to follow back out of the cave. After pausing a moment more, the train backed up, and we returned as we had entered. Then we were standing outside again, in the glistening sunlight of southern France.

I see now that my journey through grief was as dark as that cave beneath the earth. I had feared the beast that I might find there—the terrible mirror of my own pain and anguish. The deeper I went, the darker the cave had become—so dark that when I turned to look back, I could no longer see where I began. And the ending lay so hidden, unknown, and far away that my vision could not encompass it.

But in the end my journey taught me that the path can go on and on, even in the bleakest cave; that sometimes you will see Ariadne's thread, and sometimes, in the darkness, you cannot; but you must persevere in the hope that there will be light. That is the journey. That is the search. You are not lost, after all.

8

WHAT IS LOST
IS FOUND

I<small>T WAS ONE</small> of those sultry June evenings in Baltimore, with
heat rising hazily from the pavement. Then the clouds burst,
the rain poured down, and my brothers and I stepped outside
the shelter of the synagogue, into the summer mist.

Jeffrey, Ronnie, and I had gone to the Friday night Sabbath service with a purpose, to recite the mourner's *Kaddish* on the fifteenth anniversary of our mother's death.
It had been a coincidence that I would be in town that evening—in the hometown I had left shortly after Mom's death.
For the first time since that first year, we sat huddled beside each other, "the Cole children," remembering our
mother. Now we all had children of our own, none of whom
had ever met their grandmother except in the imagination of
their parents.

Shivering from the rain despite the heat, I looked up and
said, "It's hard to believe it's been fifteen years, isn't it?"

"Fifteen years," Jeffrey repeated, his voice reflecting the
dazed wonder I felt.

Then Ronnie nodded and said, "Mom would have liked it

that we were all together tonight. She would have liked that a lot."

In the car, I watched the rain splatter across the windshield and along the neat, wide suburban streets that part of me had never left. Jeffrey and Ronnie lived only a mile apart from each other and another mile from where our father still lived, in the big white house where we had grown up. The green leaves rustled in the summer rain, and for a moment I dreamed that when we arrived at Jeffrey's home for the traditional Sabbath dinner that we used to celebrate each Friday night at Mom's table, we would be greeted not only by our father and all our children but by our mother, too.

That did not happen, of course, but when we pulled into the driveway, walked into the bustling dining room, and sat down, I knew that our presence together this evening truly was Mom's legacy to us. Here were her children and grandchildren, all sitting at a table to observe the Sabbath traditions that she had taught us to observe in her home so many years before. Her granddaughters lit the shining Sabbath candles, then Jeffrey held the silver wine cup and chanted the Friday night *kiddush* in the same off-key tune of his that I remembered from long ago.

Nothing more was said about Mom at the table that night; perhaps nothing more had to be said. My sister-in-law had made the spicy mashed potatoes—Jeffrey's favorite dish all through his growing up—whose recipe Mom had given her as an engagement gift. Even before we could dig in, the two oldest grandchildren, both named for Mom—Ronnie's son, Ryan, and Jeffrey's daughter Debra Rachel—had started bubbling excitedly about their latest interests and activities. The conversation drifted from sports to politics to interior design, and inwardly I thought: how delighted Mom would have been with the pleasure we all so clearly took in her grandchildren's delight; with Ryan and Debra, effervescent with preteen energy; with their sisters, Lori and Heather, each aged ten, who picked daintily at their food and shyly giggled at their secret jokes; with my little Edward, at six-

199

teen months the youngest at the table, and with Edward's twenty-one-month-old cousin, Steven, as they intently studied, signaled, and babbled to each other in high-pitched squeals that only they could grasp.

Then Jeffrey announced a special treat: Did we remember the old home movies Dad used to take? They had become so worn that to preserve them, Jeffrey had transferred them to video. He had spliced the old films together with newer ones, so that each videocassette covered many different chapters in our family's life.

This particular cassette begins nineteen years ago: Here are Jeffrey and his bride-to-be, Linda, at their college graduation, waving their rolled diplomas in the air. And there, beaming beside them in her favorite mint-green dress, is Mom —smiling, squinting into the bright summer sun while at the same time blinking away the moisture from her light-hazel eyes.

The images roll forward. "Look, Edward," I say, pointing excitedly to a heavyset gentleman with eyebrows thick as hairbrushes, bravely wearing in the frailty of old age the shadow of his once hearty grin. "That's your great-grandfather, for whom you were named!" And even though I know he cannot understand, I point and point again, and Edward smiles at my smile.

Now the scene changes, and here is Mom again, this time leaning gently forward over Linda's dark-eyed infant nephew to ooh and coo: a poignant glimpse of the adoring embrace her own grandchildren would miss but that we supply instead in imagination as Jeffrey rewinds the scene and plays it again and again, as if repetition alone can bring the figure on the screen back to life.

The film moves on, the years pass. We're at Jeffrey's wedding . . . a summer vacation in Cape Cod . . . and then Jeffrey's medical school graduation, just three weeks before Mom's death. "Jeff—are you sure you want to play this?" my sister-in-law asks, adding as she looks at me, "It's very painful—your mother so weak—" But it's Ronnie who answers, feel himself to be out of step with his contemporaries and perhaps with the world. Perhaps I never would be precisely in sync or in step with others' music again, but I must attempt now, as I had before, to find my own harmony and beat. I had played one melody on the flute, and I had heard another in these lyrics by Emily Dickinson. And even though I did not yet know what theme I would hear next, perhaps, someday, that music would include the songs of children, my children.

"Because. Why not?" As I left the concert hall that afternoon, I remembered Peter's answer from long ago and heard in it this time a more specific meaning: Why not see the music through not just to its end but to the possibility of a new beginning, whatever that beginning might be?

I had listened further, and I had seen that, without knowing it, I had already begun to prepare for those next notes. By then Peter and I had redecorated our home in such a way that my old study—the room that was to have been our baby's room—was left suspended in a kind of limbo, as an extra den. Slowly it had become a storage room, its closet filled with my maternity clothes, a place to store our future dreams as well as those that had died. This room, filled equally with sad reminders and with poignant hope, was a part of my home, a part of my life. But in the same way that there can be a break in the music, a rest between movements, I saw that even if I closed this room's door for a time, glancing within only now and then, I could still live in the other rooms of my home, and in the rest of my life.

As I imagined the music of my life unfolding, I also saw that, eventually, I would clean out that room and make it a new room—whether a child's room or a different kind of room, I did not yet know. But I would be content to wait out the music, for life had also taught me that there were notes and turns in every song that no one could predict.

Now, lying in bed in Baltimore, I heard a faint whimper from Edward through the bedroom wall. The groan faded sleepily as Edward turned and went back to sleep, but the sound of his cry brought back the memory of his arrival and how, from the moment I first cradled him, I knew he was the child I had yearned for all those years. It had struck me then that the road that had brought him into my life had begun with loss, but it had led to joy. Perhaps the words I had spoken to my niece also applied to me. Mom had not lived to see this legacy, but the presence of her memory would nurture us all.

It had been fifteen years since Mom's death, more than sixteen since Peter's surgery, and that, too, had left its legacy. How odd, I thought: Peter's external scars will remain outwardly visible for the rest of his life, yet in a certain way even these had long since become imperceptible both to Peter and to me. They had become so unnoted in their familiarity that after the ectopic pregnancy, I had pointed to the narrow pink abdominal scar the surgeon's knife had left on me and asked Peter if the surgical blemish bothered him. Peter had stared at me for a long moment before we both laughed out loud—the laughter of recognition. We both had scars, that laughter proclaimed, and though those marks might in some form remain with us forever, they also would heal and become almost invisible, unless we looked for them.

Now I gazed in memory at all those scars, and I saw reflected in them a map of our losses, but I also saw a map of the journey we had taken to arrive where we were. It was a home filled with a child's laughter and his parents' joy—after great pain, a new life.